"If You Could Hear
What I Cannot Say"

Learning to Communicate
with the Ones You Love

OTHER BOOKS BY NATHANIEL BRANDEN

WHO IS AYN RAND?

THE PSYCHOLOGY OF SELF-ESTEEM

BREAKING FREE

THE DISOWNED SELF

A NATHANIEL BRANDEN ANTHOLOGY
    (includes *The Psychology of Self-Esteem, Breaking Free,*
    and *The Disowned Self*)

THE PSYCHOLOGY OF ROMANTIC LOVE

THE ROMANTIC LOVE QUESTION & ANSWER BOOK
    (with E. Devers Branden)

"If You Could Hear What I Cannot Say"

Learning to Communicate with the Ones You Love

Nathaniel Branden

BANTAM BOOKS
Toronto · New York · London · Sydney

Bantam Books are published by Bantam Books, Inc. Its trade-
mark, consisting of the words "Bantam Books" and the por-
trayal of a rooster, is Registered in U.S. Patent and Trademark
Office and in other countries. Marca Registrada. Bantam
Books, Inc., 666 Fifth Avenue, New York, New York 10103.

PRINTED IN THE UNITED STATES OF AMERICA

0 9 8 7 6 5 4 3 2 1

ACKNOWLEDGMENTS

I want to express my deep appreciation and gratitude to my wife and colleague, Devers Branden, who assisted me in virtually every phase of this book—conceptually, editorially, and in the selection of case illustrations—and whose cheerful good humor helped me to persevere when the project turned out to be far more complicated than I had initially imagined.

My thanks to my friend, Allan Jay Friedman, who, after witnessing a demonstration of sentence-completion work, proposed the idea of writing this book.

My thanks for the assistance of Linda Cunningham, my editor at Bantam, and Ann Poe, my copy editor, both of whom made many valuable suggestions concerning the final structuring and organizing of this material.

My thanks to Karl Stull for his editorial help and suggestions in the first draft of this book.

And finally, my thanks to Nancie Gilbert, who carefully and conscientiously typed and retyped the many versions of this book on the way to its present form.

Contents

Preface

The essence of relationships is communication. And yet, even between people who care deeply for each other, communication sometimes becomes blocked. We cannot put our feelings into words. Our partner speaks, but we do not hear. We cry out, but no one answers. We talk, neither of us saying what needs to be said, neither of us understanding what needs to be understood, our words circling like enemies. We stare helplessly across an abyss of silence, or we hurl attacks that drive us farther and farther apart. Communication is at an impasse.

This is a book about the art of breaking through that impasse—so that alienation and estrangement are replaced by contact and intimacy.

My views on love, man/woman relationships, and the importance of effective communication are presented in *The Psychology of Romantic Love* and *The Romantic Love Question & Answer Book* (written with my wife and colleague, Devers). They represent the intellectual background of this book. Here I shall be concerned with a specific aspect of communication in intimate relationships: overcoming the barriers to self-expression and mutual understanding.

By way of establishing a context for the present discussion, I want to quote from *The Romantic Love Question & Answer Book*:

To be nurtured, then, is to experience that I am cared for. Not to be nurtured is to be deprived of the experience that I am cared for. . . .

Frustration arising from inadequate nurturing seems to be one of the most common complaints of couples, yet it is often difficult for them to talk about. They often feel uncomfortable acknowledging such a need. . . .

In our therapy and couple counseling sessions, we help couples learn the nurturing process. We may have them sit facing each other for a two-person sentence-completion exercise. One person listens attentively while the other does a string of ten or fifteen sentence completions, beginning with "One of the things I want from you and am hesitant to ask for is—." The idea is to finish the sentence several times as rapidly as possible with whatever comes to mind. Then the process is reversed; the partner who had been listening now does his or her own string of sentence completions. We then encourage the couple to explore whether or not each would be willing to provide what the other wants and, if there are barriers, whether they can be overcome. If they are willing to cooperate, the couple can begin their apprenticeship in the art of nurturing.

The sentence-completion technique originated as a tool in psychotherapy to facilitate self-discovery, self-expression, and self-healing. I found that it could be powerfully effective in assisting couples to resolve conflicts in their relationship. Soon it became apparent that couples who had grasped the essentials of the technique could use it on their own—at home without my guidance—to cut through a wide variety of communication difficulties.

I welcome the opportunity to show how the sentence completion works and at the same time respond to the requests of colleagues who have asked for more information on how I use this technique in psychotherapy and marriage counseling.

Perhaps I should emphasize at the outset that this book does not come fully into existence until the reader actively participates as coauthor by doing the exercises. Without doing the exercises, there is no way to understand what the book is teaching, let alone take advantage of the benefits sentence completion can offer in relationships (or in therapy.). This is a book not for passive spectators but for active participants who are willing to discover for themselves—*through direct experience*—how the sentence-completion process can contribute to their lives.

Sometimes self-awareness and self-expression are difficult. Sometimes intimate contact and communication with another human being are difficult. We may be afraid to face our own feelings, needs, and thoughts. We may be afraid to express them to another because of how we imagine the other may react. So we live private lives, lives that are secret from others and from ourselves.

Often the communication impasse we experience between ourselves and another person is a reflection of a communication impasse within us—our fear of hearing the voice of our deepest self.

Sentence completion is a tool to assist us in breaking free. But it can be challenging—challenging precisely because of its power, precisely because of its effectiveness. We may be reluctant to engage in it, not because we doubt it will work, but because we fear it will. It is at this point that rationalizations become tempting: "Sentence completion is artificial." "It's unnatural; no one talks that way." "It's contrived." "It's mechanical." And so forth.

But nothing is gained without courage, neither self-awareness nor intimacy with another person. If you are willing fully to participate in the exercises that follow, if you are willing fully to give yourself to them, after having studied all the guidelines presented in the first three chapters, you will have a unique opportunity to encounter in new ways an extraordinarily interesting and worthwhile human being: yourself. You will learn how to make yourself better known and understood to those you love. You will learn how to express your feelings and listen more effectively. If you follow all of these exercises through to the end of the book, you will have become more intelligent about yourself and those you deal with.

Will every problem in your personal life be answered and solved? Of course not. Will you be left with some unanswered questions? Almost certainly. Will you and your partner (if you have one) speak more honestly and openly to each other than you have in the past? Emphatically yes.

That is not all there is to success in life and romantic love, true enough. But it is a major step. Let us proceed together.

Chapter 1

The Communication Impasse

Communication is the lifeblood of any relationship, and the love relationship in particular demands communication if it is to flourish. Because of the intensity of the feelings involved, special problems in communicating emotions often arise between people in love. . . .

When dealing with couples who complain of communication difficulties, we always ask, "Do you create a context in which your partner can feel free to share feelings, thoughts, fantasies, hurts, and complaints, without the fear that you will condemn, attack, lecture, or simply withdraw? And does your partner create such a context for you?" If a couple cannot answer yes to these questions, and these couples almost never can, we need not wonder at the difficulties in their relationship.

Of course, we cannot demand of our partner that he or she applaud everything we feel, but we want and need to be able to express ourselves in an atmosphere of respect and acceptance. And it is just such an atmosphere that our partner desires and needs from us.

Before we can provide that atmosphere for another person, we must learn to create it for ourselves. If we have learned to lecture and reproach ourselves for inappropriate feelings, we almost certainly will treat others the same way. We will lecture and reproach our partner, we will lecture and reproach our children. "I never had a right to my emotions. Why should you have a right to yours?" We will encourage the person we love to practice the same self-disowning, the same self-repudiation, that we practice. "I play dead. Why can't you?" By treating each other as they treat themselves, two perfectly well-intentioned human beings can undermine and eventually destroy their happiness.

Working on a relationship always begins, therefore, with working on ourselves.

The Romantic Love Question
& Answer Book

"If we knew how to communicate," said a client in one of my group therapy sessions, "I wonder if we would be here."

"Sometimes I wonder if I know what communication means," said her husband.

Another client joined in. "What I don't understand is why it should be so difficult so often."

"Communication means different things to different people," said someone else.

"I'd like to do a little work with open-ended sentences," I said to the twelve men and women sitting in a circle in my office. "Let's go around with the phrase **Communication to me means—**. Repeat the sentence stem and add your own ending. If you feel stuck or have nothing to say, invent. Let's keep the momentum going." I tapped the knee of the man on my immediate left. "Will you begin? **Communication to me means—**"

"Communication to me means . . . being able to put my feelings into words."

"Communication to me means . . . being listened to and understood," said the next person in the circle.

Each person repeated the stem and added a new ending as his or her turn came up. Here are the endings proposed about the meaning of communication:

not being afraid I'll be criticized
or jumped on for whatever comes out of my mouth.

having my statements acknowledged by the listener.

neither of us responding with ridicule.

communicating feelings of pain, anger, or fear without my partner
withdrawing or attacking.

really being listened to.

having my partner try to understand
my intention, even if I'm not expressing myself perfectly.

touching.

both parties feeling free to be honest about thoughts and feelings.

staying with the issues.

being asked to explain when something isn't clear.

two people really looking at each other, seeing each other, hearing each other, really being present.

empathy and compassion.

*having the right to say everything
you need to say, and giving the same right to your partner.*

*the willingness not to shut down,
the determination to stay open and receptive.*

being able to listen to criticism without becoming defensive.

being solution-oriented, not revenge-oriented.

conveying interest in and understanding of each other's feelings.

being willing to be visible to each other.

not playing games—just saying what you mean.

being intimate.

*being determined to come to an understanding no matter how long
it takes.*

not resorting to abuse.

treating all expressions of feelings with respect.

*knowing how to put yourself in the other person's shoes at times
and being willing to do it.*

*getting a response that's appropriate in terms of what you've said, a
real answer.*

*arriving at a shared perception
of the situation, seeing the same
reality.*

coming to some conclusion or solution.

Each of their responses touched on one aspect of effective communication. Each answer was right. Doubtless the person volunteering a particular answer emphasized something that had significant personal charge or meaning. Taken together, their responses articulate a fairly comprehensive list. Reviewing the list, we can begin to see what people want from communication and how they are often frustrated.

If you are in a relationship at present and are experiencing communication difficulties, the above list of items can be helpful. They can help you to see what you and your partner may not be giving to or receiving from each other. Looked at from that perspective, each item is a potential springboard for a discussion that may clarify and help remedy some of your communication difficulties.

Any number of fights, quarrels, hurts, and misunderstandings arises out of just the kind of issues raised by these items. Obviously, without good will, without a genuine effort to understand what may be getting in the way of you and your partner, a discussion of these items is unlikely to be fruitful. But if there is good will and the desire to understand, there could hardly be a better place to begin than with a joint examination of this list from the standpoint of the light it might throw on your conversational transactions.

"But I don't see why it should be so difficult," said the man who had raised the issue earlier, "considering how obviously important communication is."

"When it comes to sharing intimate thoughts, feelings, wants, and needs, just about everybody I know gets stuck. Me in particular," said a woman.

I listened silently for a few minutes while individuals in the circle volunteered their thoughts and feelings about the difficulty of achieving mutual understanding in an intimate relationship.

I decided to take advantage of the fact that I was working with a group that day to explore further the issue of why people get "stuck." One of the advantages of group is the amount of input an individual can receive from a variety of sources during a relatively short time.

I said, "Let's work with the sentence stem **The hard thing about intimate communication is—**." Again, I tapped the person on my left, gesturing for the group to keep going round with that stem until I signaled a stop.

The hard thing about intimate communication is—

I'm afraid of how my partner will react.

so many thoughts and feelings start whirling around in my head, I don't know where to start. I choke up.

words scare me.

talking only seems to make things
worse.

he only pretends to listen. What's
the use?

I'm sick and tired of being criticized.
I got enough of that when I was a child.
I just don't want to hear anything.

if my partner knew how much anger
I've got inside me, that would be
that. He would turn away from me.

if I start letting my pain out,
it would never end.

I don't want to be laughed at.

I don't want to admit I have needs and wants.
It makes me too vulnerable.

I hate having to ask for what I want.
It's humiliating.

if there were real love between us,
talk wouldn't be necessary.
I know that's ridiculous.

when I open up, my partner can hurt me.

if I admit fear or pain, it will be seen as weakness.

if I start talking about something bothering me, my partner comes back
with reproaches. I prefer silence.

no one cares about what I want; no one ever has. Why should that change
now?

I don't want to be told I am foolish.

I'm never really clear, and if people don't like what they think I said,
I can always claim I said something else.

I don't know what's relevant to tell and what isn't.

I just feel blocked, mentally and emotionally.

I'm scared of my own rage.

I begin to feel angry and then my mind goes blank.

Given the prevalence of these attitudes—and they are very prevalent—small wonder so many love relationships that begin with hope and excitement end in despair and alienation. If communication is the lifeboood of a relationship, attitudes such as these block the flow of shared perceptions and understandings that rejuvenate love.

You have just witnessed two simple examples of how sentence-completion work can be done in a group setting. It can be done in a wide variety of ways, as you will see in the course of this book. But the essential idea is always that a person is given an open-ended sentence or sentence stem and asked to keep providing new endings.

The individual is encouraged to say whatever comes to mind, without worrying whether each ending is literally true or whether any particular ending conflicts with any other. Spontaneity is more important than literalness in this context. The freedom to say whatever springs to mind is essential.

These points will be demonstrated in the stories presented below. Experience has taught me that it is very difficult to explain the sentence-completion technique in the abstract. The best way to understand its power is to experience it in action. And perhaps the best way to begin is as an observer—a witness to the way in which others use sentence completion to expand self-awareness, break through communication barriers, and resolve conflicts.

To understand and master the technique fully, of course, you must become an active participant, as I have already indicated, but for the next little while you are invited to imagine that you are an invisible observer at some therapy sessions where sentence completion is being used.

Nothing is asked of you at present but to sit back, relax, and allow the following stories to unfold. If you are willing to do that, learning will happen.

Phyllis and Paul had come for counseling in the sixteenth year of their marriage, a time when Phyllis was seriously considering divorce. In fact, it was only the prospect of divorce that made Paul willing to consult a psychotherapist.

The near death of their son in a traffic accident precipitated the crisis that brought them to my office. For sixteen years Phyllis said she had lived with a man who had little capacity for conversation outside the context of business. He showed no interest in his own feelings or anyone else's, no grasp of the meaning of emotional intimacy. She admired him in many ways, but found their relationship unbearably arid. For nine days, while their son was in the hospital, the doctor could not be certain whether the boy would sustain permanent brain damage. Paul was there every day and asked all the right questions of the medical staff, but he displayed no emotion of any kind and no particular concern for the emotional condition of his wife. Once their son was out of danger and on the way to recovery, Phyllis felt unwilling and unable to go on with their life as before.

"I put up with it for years because I loved him and knew he loved me in his own way. But it's like living in a desert. No nourishment. I'm starving. Paul is a good human being, but goodness isn't enough. I need someone to talk to. Someone who's interested in what's happening inside of me. But he's not even interested in what's happening inside himself."

While she said this, Paul looked miserable. He remained silent, as if the sole responsibility for communication were hers.

When I asked for his reaction to what his wife was saying, he shook his head. "I don't want a divorce. I want us to go on living together."

I asked him why. His answer was interesting in its indirection.

"I've never loved anyone else."

"And do you love Phyllis?"

"That's why I'm here. I'll do anything."

His love for his wife was apparently genuine, but it was equally apparent that he was cut off from his own feelings. I remarked that sometimes people had things they badly needed to express and really wanted to express, yet didn't quite know how.

"That's right," Paul nodded.

This was their first day in therapy. After the sentence-completion exercise on communication, in the group of which they were the newest members, Phyllis asked if they might begin to work on their problem.

I had them sit facing each other in the center of the group, and I asked them to spend a moment or two looking into each other's eyes. Making eye contact is a step toward intimacy, or it can be, just as avoiding eye contact is one of the most obvious ways of avoiding intimacy. Paul and Phyllis were to experience whatever they were feeling, without the need to say or do anything.

"Now, Phyllis, your part in this exercise will be to listen to what Paul has to say. Listen not only with your ears but with your whole being. Listen the way so many of us want to be listened to and so rarely are. See him, really see him. Don't answer; don't respond. Just be there. Hear what Paul has to say."

Then I said to Paul, "I'm going to give you a phrase, a sentence stem, and I would like you to keep repeating my stem adding a new ending each time so as to express a complete sentence. It really doesn't matter what you say; it doesn't even matter whether each ending is literally true or false. If you get stuck or your mind goes blank, invent. Say anything. Are you willing to do that?"

Paul looked apprehensive, but he nodded.

"Good. **Ever since I was a boy—**. Keep repeating that phrase, adding a new ending each time, until I give you a different stem. All right? **Ever since I was a boy—**"

"Ever since I was a boy," Paul began. He hesitated, then looked at me. "This is really difficult."

"Please stay with Phyllis. Don't turn to me, and please don't comment on what you're doing. Just do it."

"Ever since I was a boy . . . I've been lonely."

"Good. But don't stop. Keep going."

"The same beginning again?" He shifted uncomfortably in his chair. "Ever since I was a boy . . . I've wondered. Ever since I as a boy. . . I had to be strong. Ever since I was a boy, there was no time and no chance to be a boy." Paul turned to me. "That's doesn't make sense."

"Please don't comment or criticize what you say. Stay with Phyllis. Keep going."

"Ever since I was a boy, I knew a man had to stand on his own two feet."

I introduced a new stem: **"Father was always—"**

"Father was always strong. Father was always working. Father was always not there. Father was always distant. Father was always quiet. Father was always controlled."

"What I wanted from Father and never got was—"

"What I wanted from Father and never got was affection. What I wanted from Father and never got was warmth. What I wanted from Father and never got was a smile."

At last he was looking at Phyllis as he gave these endings.

If I were to admit how much I care about our son—

I wouldn't know where to begin.

I'd cry for a month.

I'd tell you how scared I was when he was in the hospital.

I'd admit I was in terror.

I'd admit my terror was worse than anything I can say.

I'd start crying right now.

I'd wonder what you'd think of me.

I'd lose control.

I'd make you feel there was no one strong for you to lean on.

I'd tell you how hard it was when I was a little boy. I could never tell my father.

Paul's eyes were moist. Tears were flowing from Phyllis's eyes.

"Rest for a moment," I said. "Breathe deeply. Just allow whatever you're feeling to be there. Notice it. No words." After a moment, I said, "Let's continue. That's all right, Paul. Just allow that trembling to be there. **If the child in me could speak, he might tell you—**"

I'm not allowed to speak.

I want someone to see me.

I want someone to tell me it's all right.

I don't want to grow up yet.

I need time.

I love you.

I love you very much.

I want to. . . to reach out. I want to reach you.

If I could tell you how much I love you—

I'd cry and cry and cry.

I'd break down.

you'd know.

I'd be ashamed to admit my need.

I'd wonder what else I might say.

I think I could relax a little.

I think our whole marriage would change.

you'd understand me.

I'd understand you.

everything . . . our whole . . . everything would be different.

These endings eloquently signified a shift in Paul's state of being, apparent to everyone in the room. His face had softened, and he looked younger. His eyes were shining with a new and gentle clarity.

"Okay, ease up for a minute." Next I asked him to go with **One of the things I appreciate about you is**—

who you are.

your strength.

your thoughtfulness.

your intelligence.

the way you are with our son.

your love for me.

your patience.

your body.

your patience and your loyalty.

Phyllis's expression made it clear she could hardly believe this was happening.

When I asked Paul what he was feeling, he smiled. "Light. And also a little light-headed."

Then it was Paul's turn to be the one who listened quietly while Phyllis talked. Phyllis followed the same procedure, repeating the stem and putting on a different ending each time.

As I sit here listening to you—

I could burst.

I feel confused.

I see how hard you're trying.

I don't know what to make of all of this.

I feel loved.

I wonder if this is real.

I love your courage.

I'm wondering how to take what's happening.

I feel there's hope.

I'm hearing you talk as you've never talked before.

I'm wondering why it's coming so easily.

It's a miracle.

I feel your pain.

I feel your fear.

I congratulated each of them on how well they had done. Then I said, "It's really hard to give another person what we can't first give ourselves. If I am not allowed to feel my own pain, how can I respond appropriately to yours? If I don't permit myself to feel my own fear, how can I understand yours? It's not easy to treat you better or more wisely than I treat myself."

Phyllis nodded with compassion and recognition. Paul began to sob quietly while Phyllis held him. Afterward Paul remarked, his face softer and years younger, "I don't believe I've ever cried in anyone's arms in my whole life, not since I was a little boy."

At the end of the session they were given a homework assignment: to participate in the "intimacy marathon" described in *The Psychology of Romantic Love* and *The Romantic Love Question & Answer Book*. In essence a couple agrees to spend a day together, twelve hours, entirely alone. No books, no television, no telephone calls— no distractions of any kind. If they have children, they call someone to take care of them. The couple is committed to remaining together in the same room with breaks only for meals and bathroom visits. They further agree that no matter what the other might say, neither will leave the room refusing to talk. They can sit for several hours in total and absolute silence if they like, but they must remain together. And there must be no physical violence, no matter what either party says. They are free during this twelve-hour session to talk about anything, providing it is personal. No talk of business, the children's schoolwork, redecorating the living room, or any other such subjects. They must talk about themselves or each other or their relationship. They have only themselves. This situation tends to open doors to intimacy. (Sometimes, not often, the first effort at a twelve-hour intimacy marathon seems to end in a debacle; there is more chaos and confusion than clarity and contact. I cannot think of a single instance in my experience, however, where the second twelve-hour session did not break the impasse. The first effort was not a failure but a necessary precondition for the subsequent breakthrough.)

For Phyllis and Paul, the twelve-hour intimacy marathon was a frightening and exhilarating experience—frightening because neither of them knew where intimacy might lead, exhilarating because they found it led them back to each other.

Here is another vignette concerning a communication impasse, and another example of the way sentence completion works if you are willing to use it.

"From making love almost every night," said Walter, "we went to two or three times a week, to once a week, to once every ten days. Now maybe we make love twice a month."

"Walter talks as if the only problem is sex," said Jacqueline, "It isn't. It's everything."

"What else is wrong?" Walter asked her.

Instead of replying, she said to me, "We try to talk. We don't know what to say, I don't know why we waited so long to come for counseling. The strangest kind of lethargy seems to have taken over both of us. It's almost as if we were drugged. The days and months and years pass, and the full awareness of what's wrong doesn't penetrate. Work used to be a help and a distraction. Not anymore."

"Everything has gone stale," said Walter. "And we don't know why."

"Then you admit that it's not just sex," Jacqueline said.

Walter sighed. "I guess not. We're . . . not connecting anymore, we're out of contact."

"You act as if I were the one who had withdrawn sexually," said Jacqueline, a shade irritably. "You're fully as withdrawn as I am."

"I thought we just agreed," said Walter, "that the problem is more than sexual."

Jacqueline directed her next statement to me. "I can't imagine doing sentence-completion work. I know you've explained it, but I just can't. It seems so artificial. Couldn't we just talk?"

"We have been talking," said Walter. "It never leads anywhere. Like right now."

They had been married eight years, and both were highly career-oriented. He was a lawyer; she was an account executive at a brokerage house. They were both in their thirties, attractive, energetic, and dispirited.

The only enthusiasm they seemed to have left was tennis, which they played several times a week. Their time after work was filled with an active social life. Their vacations always included at least one other couple. Neither could remember the last time they spent a weekend together, just the two of them.

Now, sitting side by side facing me, they looked hurt and angry, but neither chose to speak about that. They sat, as if poised for combat.

"It isn't that we don't appreciate the importance of communication," Walter volunteered. "In the beginning we talked all the time. Talked and made love. Is it possible we've just run out of things to say?"

"I doubt that very much," I answered.

"I'm willing to try anything," said Jacqueline, "but please, no sentence completion."

"Let's make the attempt. In fact, let's begin with your aversion. Begin with the stem **The bad thing about sentence completion is—.**"

She laughed. "Oh, hell, you're determined to trap me, aren't you?"

"In a manner of speaking, you hired me to trap you."

"True."

When they sat facing each other, I repeated to Jacqueline, **"The bad thing about sentence completion is—."**

"The bad thing about sentence completion is it's phony." She turned to me. "I really feel uncomfortable doing this."

"Are you willing to continue?"

"The bad thing about sentence completion is . . . it's artificial . . . no one talks this way . . . I can't do it and I wonder if—"

"Please keep your sentences short snd simple."

"The bad thing about sentence completion is I might reveal too much." Nervously, but looking steadily now at Walter, she went on. **The bad thing about sentence completion is—**

I don't know what I might say.

I'm out of control.

you might get angry at me.

I might lose my cool.

Mother always said, "Don't rock the boat."

my throat gets tight.

I feel self-conscious.

something wants to come out.

One of the things I'd like you to know about me is—

I'm scared.

I can feel my heart beating.

I love you.

I don't want our marriage to bust up.

I think you're the sexiest man I've ever known.

I don't know where all my feelings have gone to.

this exercise makes me feel trapped and suffocated.

It was time to take off some of the pressure. Clearly, certain statements and feelings wanted and needed to come out, but the thought of that happening frightened her. To help Jacqueline along, I brought Walter into the exercise as an active participant: "Over to you now. Go with the stem **One of the things I'd like you to know about me is—**"

I'm scared, too.

I'm smart.

I'm aggressive.

I work hard.

I really like to do a good job for my clients.

I admire your success.

I'm proud of your good looks.

I sometimes wonder what's it all for.

looking into your eyes and talking this way is very exciting.

I don't want to be without you.

I'm in love with you.

I can feel myself coming closer and then withdrawing every other second.

As he spoke, he took her hands in his and smiled warmly and reassuringly, as if to say, "See? It's safe."

To give him the opportunity to explore his own fears (and possibly hers) more fully, I gave him the stem **The scary thing about this is—**

I don't know what I'll say.

I have to keep going.

I'm not on top of things.

you might not like it.

you might find out I'm not so strong.

you might see my insecurities.

we might reconnect.

you might start feeling warmer toward me.

I might . . . saying these things makes me feel how important you are,

how much I need you.

Then Jacqueline completed the same stem, **The scary thing about this is—**

I don't like surprises.

I wish we could just be happy again.

sometimes I suspect I'm crazy.

suppose my craziness comes out?

suppose I scare you.

suppose I'm not what you think.

suppose neither of us is what we think.

I want to be married to you.

I introduced a stem that seemed to bear no relationship to what either of them had been saying. If my hypothesis about Jacqueline was valid, something inside of her would know how to make the transition. I gave her the stem **If you knew how much anger I have locked up inside of me—.**

On a subconscious level she made the connection. She picked up the sentence stem without missing a beat. **If you knew how much anger I have locked up inside of me—**

you wouldn't believe it was me.

you'd run for your life.

I can't imagine ever telling you.

I wonder how you'd react.

I wonder how I'd react.

it's not fair.

I would be stupid.

I'd disgust you.

you would wonder if . . . I would wonder if I was sane.

Walter listened attentively, as if he, too, saw the connection that neither of them had been able to put into words before. I said to him, "Go with the same stem. **If you knew how much anger I have locked up inside of me—**"

you'd be shocked.

you'd be surprised.

you wouldn't believe it.

you might not be surprised at all.

you'd be scared.

you'd want to run out of here.

you'd be frightened to live with me.

would anything be left?

you'd wonder what had happened to Walter.

you'd think, Who needs this?

I asked them to pause, breathe, relax into their feelings, and continue looking at each other without words. They were visibly agitated. Their breathing was shaky, and their bodies were trembling. "Just allow that," I said to them. "Try not to fight what you're experiencing. It's good. It means you're waking up."

I wanted to create an atmosphere of acceptance in which they could acknowledge their anger without a sense of catastrophe. In a nonchalant manner, I said to Walter, "Let's go with another stem. **One of the things I'm angry about is—**"

I don't like working so hard.

I resent what's happened to our sex life.

everything I do ends up being an effort.

we're always running.

I feel sexually rejected.

you don't see when I'm trying to reach out to you.

when I try to talk, you find ways to change the subject.

you don't turn on to me the way you used to.

you never notice when I'm tired.

you're just like my mother—expecting! expecting! expecting!

At this point Walter appeared hurt, angry, stunned, distressed. I asked him to pause and to breathe into his feelings. Hoping to engage Jacqueline in the momentum Walter had generated, I said to her, "Let's go. Same stem. **One of the things I'm angry about is—.**"

Instead of shifting into sentence completion, Jacqueline began speaking almost incoherently about her grievances against Walter. Her rage seemed directed against both of us.

"I can see that you're very angry," I said to her, "and I want you to have a chance to express that anger and put into words what you're angry about. Your anger is important, your pain is important, and I think Walter and I both want to hear about it. Let sentence completion help."

One of the things I'm angry about is—

you don't want a wife, you want an audience!

I don't appeal to you sexually anymore!

you never listen!

you punish me by sexual withdrawal!

if I were crying, you wouldn't notice!

you remind me of my father!

Mother always said, "It's a man's world!"

you resent my vitality!

if I begin to get angry, your eyes run away!

I don't know how to get angry!

I'm angry, and I don't know what to do with it!

Another pause for breathing deeply, experiencing their feelings, relinquishing words.

Walter grinned. Jacqueline laughed a bit nervously.

"This is fantastic," she said to Walter, intimately, almost as if I were not present.

"This is exciting," Walter agreed.

"Thank you," said Jacqueline, looking at me. "God, what a release that was!"

One of the premises underlying sentence-completion work is that we know more than we are immediately aware of; the subconscious is very often far ahead of the conscious in its understanding. The problem Walter and Jacqueline raised had not yet come explicitly into focus. The elements of the problem were being drawn out through their sentence completions. At this point there was no need to hasten the process: the more that came from them and the less that came from me, the better.

I allowed myself only one general observation. "Sometimes when we repress hurt and anger, we repress other feelings as well. When we numb ourselves to our negative feelings, there's no way to avoid numbing ourselves to our positive feelings at the same time—because what we are really doing is numbing ourselves to all feelings. Relationships don't flourish when people try to preserve them by making themselves dead. That's why ignoring grievances can be dangerous."

All clients in therapy with me are asked to bring tape recorders and record their work (just as you will be advised to use a tape recorder if you do the exercises in this book aloud with a partner). Sometimes I ask them to make complete transcripts to facilitate the process of absorption and assimilation. Walter and Jacqueline agreed to listen to their tape at least four times before our next session. In addition, I gave them a homework exercise. They were to work together with these sentence stems:

Sometimes I feel hurt when you—

Sometimes I feel angry when you—

Sometimes when I'm hurt I—

Sometimes when I'm angry I—

Two sessions later, Jacqueline announced, "We've been getting a lot off our chests these past couple of weeks. The things we said in group were just the tip of the iceberg. Okay, we've both got a lot of anger and resentment, stuff we didn't deal with that has accumulated over the years. Talking helps. We're beginning to feel more connected. Sex is getting exciting again. But I still feel confused and frightened a lot of the time, and I still don't really feel I know what to do with all this anger."

Walter said, "I can't stand the explosive atmosphere we're living in, never knowing when the volcano is going to erupt—hers or mine or both. It's not my idea of marital happiness."

I asked them to sit facing each other, preparatory to working further with sentence completion.

Jacqueline protested. "Why are we always doing sentence-completion work? I know you have so many other ways of working with people."

"As I recall," I answered, "this is the second time you'll be doing sentence completion. And I'm asking you to do it because it's one of my favorite ways of showing people how much they know that they don't think they know."

"You said you would never do sentence completions," Walter observed, "and look what happened last time."

"And I still say I can't do them." But she smiled.

"Good," I said. "Walter, you'll be listener and receiver. Jacqueline, you'll do the talking at first. Begin with the stem **Sometimes when I feel angry with you—**."

I smile.

I don't hear you when you call me.

I'm not in the mood for sex.

I refuse orgasm.

I get depressed and wonder what's happening to my life and if I'll ever . . .

I feel afraid.

I wonder what you would do if I started screaming.

I bump into things.

I get awkward.

I hide.

I withdraw.

I look at you without seeing you.

I listen to you without hearing you.

If I were to express my anger honestly and straightforwardly—

I'd respect myself.

I'd be frightened.

you'd respect me.

you'd be scared.

you'd be confused.

I'd feel cleaner.

we'd become closer.

we could be friends.

sex would be the way it used to be.

I asked her to say the last sentence again, both stem and ending. The request surprised her, as if she had been tripped in the middle of a dead run. Her sentence completion, as she heard herself repeat each word, surprised her even more: "If I were to express my anger honestly and straightforwardly, sex would be the way it used to be." Her look at Walter and then at me showed that Jacqueline understood, consciously now. She had tripped on something worth a second look. Later, there would be time to reflect on this discovery.

For now, she continued with the stem. **If I were to express my anger honestly and straightforwardly—**

you'd know what's really bothering me.

we could talk about things sanely.

I'd give you a chance.

you wouldn't feel so overwhelmed.

"Pause," I said. "Walter, over to you. **Sometimes when I feel angry with you—**"

I withdraw.

I disappear inside myself.

I sulk.

I forget things you've asked me to do.

THE
COMMUNICATION
IMPASSE

I turn off sexually.

I get annoyed over trivia.

I flirt.

I think women are impossible, just as Father said.

Walter was given the stem that had proven so useful for Jacqueline. **If I were to express my anger honestly and straightforwardly—**

I'd feel how much I love you.

you'd feel how much I love you.

we wouldn't keep running around in circles.

we'd reach an understanding.

we'd see none of it is such a big deal.

we could relax.

maybe you'd get angry back.

maybe you couldn't handle it.

maybe you could handle it.

maybe you'd be happier.

maybe you'd laugh and say, "Is that all?"

maybe I'd see I've been a fool.

I believe we could enjoy each other again.

it might get rough for a while, but I think in the end it would be great.

we'd have to have the nerve to hang in there.

we'd be happy and alive again.

At this point, Jacqueline and Walter had learned a great deal about the nature of their communication impasse and about their feelings of estrangement and alienation. Sentence completion had taken them to some root causes of their problems with extraordinary speed. I did not have to interpret; I did not have to explain; I did not have to try to persuade them of anything. There was no need for an all-wise authority figure. There was merely the need for a guide—and a method—to help them make contact with knowledge already within them. Blocking hurts and grievances, denying thoughts and feelings rather than expressing them, had had a devastating and numbing effect on their relationship. What they began to see was that expression was the beginning of the way out—expression and honesty and courage.

I gave them a moment to meditate on the meaning of the things each of them had been saying. The look in their eyes said that they heard and understood. Now it was time to begin moving toward integration (assimilation and absorption), the process of pulling together and making explicit that which was only implicit in what they had said so far.

I asked Jacqueline to work with this stem. **Sex began to go wrong when—**

I felt hurt and didn't talk about it.

I bottled up my resentment.

I tried to tell myself, "You're married now. What do you expect?"

I didn't tell you about the little ways I felt ignored and neglected.

I didn't tell you when I felt put down.

I smiled when I felt angry.

I saw I could get back at you by withdrawing.

I gestured to Walter for his answers. **Sex began to go wrong when—**

I decided I wasn't going to let you hurt me.

I felt you were neglecting me in favor of work.

I told myself, Don't complain.

I ran off to play tennis rather than tell you what was bothering me.

we spent too much time with other people.

I told myself not to be petty when I was hurt.

you always seem so self-sufficient, as if you don't need anything from me.

I saw you disappearing behind your smile.

I felt I always had to be strong.

I made myself numb, not to feel pain.

"Pause," I said. "What are you experiencing now, Jacqueline?"

"Walter's last statement really hits home. That's me, too. 'Sex began to go wrong when I made myself numb, not to feel pain.' "

I asked Jacqueline to work with the stem **I'm beginning to suspect—**

when you turn off the ability to feel hurt, you turn off the ability to feel passion.

when I didn't talk about my anger, it was a crime against both of us.

I know perfectly well what to do with my anger—and so do you.

I've been afraid to make waves.

I haven't been thinking very clearly.

I haven't admitted how much I want your approval.

I've been scared of your leaving me.

I've been thinking that anger means abandonment.

I'm feeling better.

I'm feeling happier.

I really love you.

we're going to survive all this.

No matter how estranged we feel, we know we love each other.

I don't feel estranged.

we've been waiting for each other to give permission.

you're not my father, and I'm not your mother.

"Pause," I said. "Over to you, Walter. Same stem **I'm beginning to suspect—**"

I agree with you: you're not my mother, and I'm not your father.

I can relax.

I can get angry with you.

I don't need to get angry that much.

I need to tell you what's bothering me.

if we could just put things out there, express our feelings, say when we're hurt or upset, we wouldn't be tearing at each other so much, lashing out.

I feel so good right now.

I feel so much warmth toward you.

I like the way you're looking at me.

I love having your full attention.

you want me to listen to you this way, too.

I've got to give you that.

if we listened, we wouldn't get so angry, we wouldn't feel so hurt.

if we don't have the honesty to admit when we're hurt or angry, we'll never get back what we had sexually.

After these exchanges, Walter and Jacqueline entered into a more specific discussion of their respective grievances, the details of which do not matter here. What matters is the process of discovery, learning how silence and self-denial lead to estrangement between people who are (or were) in love with each other. When we numb ourselves against hurt and anger, we also numb ourselves against our partner. That feeling, or lack of feeling, spreads over every aspect of our life, though we tend to take more notice when we numb ourselves sexually.

"People are always saying it's natural for passion to die after a while," said Jacqueline.

"I've never believed that," I answered. "I do believe it's natural for passion to die between people who stop communicating."

"What do we do when we're on our own?" Walter asked. "When we get stuck and don't know how to begin talking, when the old blocks have come back, what do we do to get ourselves started?"

"It's inevitable: blocks in communication will sometimes happen," I said. "Sentence completion is one of the best ways to break the impasse. Sit facing each other, just as you do here, and experiment with some stems such as **Right now I am feeling—**, or **One of the things I wish you knew about me is—**, or **If you could hear what I cannot say—.**"

"And then?"

"And then, when each of you has taken a turn doing as many endings as he can for each of these stems and the other has listened openly and receptively, you will find you have created an appropriate context for discussion. You will have plenty to talk about."

THE
COMMUNICATION
IMPASSE

I trust it will be clear to the reader that this account of Jacqueline and Walter represents a small fragment from a total psychoterapeutic process. Sentence completion is hardly all there is to psychotherapy, and there were problems between Walter and Jacqueline that are outside the framework of this discussion. I offer this fragment only as an illustration of the possibilities for the sentence-completion method.

Here is a vignette of somewhat deeper complexity.

Tim was a psychotherapist who previously had been a dentist and who was now thinking of closing his private psychotherapy practice to open a stress clinic. "I guess I'm still trying to find myself," he said to me one day, a bit sheepishly. He was forty-nine years old.

He had difficulty articulating why he wanted to enter into therapy with me. At our first session he said, "It's not so much a specific problem as a general interest in personal growth." On another occasion he said, "My problem is I'm never satisfied, I never feel fulfilled." Once he said, "What I really want is the opportunity to experience how you work and learn from you." Another time he said, "The thing is I'd like to be married, I'd like to settle down, but I never can seem to find the right woman. I think that's my basic problem."

He had a boyish, good-natured air about him that many women found attractive. For the past year he had been living with an attractive woman in her thirties who professed to be in love with him. He professed to be in love with her, but that did not prevent him from having numerous outside affairs, and reporting them to his lover in torturous detail—somewhat, it seemed to me, like a bad boy who needs Mummy's forgiveness. Theoretically, they had an "open" relationship; in practical terms, he had his affairs and she remained scrupulously faithful. If she had done otherwise, he admitted, he would have been agonizingly jealous. This information came out during therapy sessions in small bits and pieces, almost incidentally, as if the growing strain between him and his lover were unrelated to his goals in therapy. "Lucy is a terrific person," he said, "and sometimes I wonder why she doesn't feel quite right as a final choice. I mean for marriage. Most of the time we get along marvelously. We're very compatible sexually. Except sometimes when we're out socially, she's a bit slow-moving for me. Oh, I don't know."

He had been married and divorced when he was young. His wife, he remarked, had been "a mother figure." He claimed to be ready now for "a mature relationship." He qualified, "At least, I think I'm ready."

Week by week, he dwelt more and more on his relationships past and present, on his need for a woman in his life, on his confusion over what kind of woman he could be happy with, and so forth. We achieved considerable clarification as to his values and needs, but there was always the sense of something elusive, something missing, something not yet confronted that underlay everything he said.

One day Tim announced, "Lucy says she'd like to come work with you. I think it's a good idea. I'd like to spend some time working on our relationship. What do you think?"

When Lucy was interviewed as to her goals in therapy, she said, "I'd like to understand my relationship with Tim and resolve it one way or the other. I'd like a commitment from him, or else I'd like to know that it's hopeliess and we're not going anywhere."

In therapy they agreed that their past efforts to discuss the relationship invariably bogged down in confusion, hurt feelings, and anger. "Lucy won't let me be me," said Tim.

"Tim doesn't know what he wants."

"Why are you always picking on me?" said Tim, sounding like a teenager who has been scolded too often.

"Don't I have a right to my feelings?" Lucy demanded, then looked away. "I don't have Tim's ease with words," she said to me. She was a dance teacher, and at times she seemed to be too impressed by Tim's academic background. "He can talk circles around me. By the time we're finished with a conversation, he can have me feeling guilty that I'm not happy with him just as he is."

"I can't make you do anything," said Tim. "That's your responsibility."

"See what I mean?" Lucy said—again, to me. "That's typical. I know Tim can't make me do anything. But he knows perectly well what I'm trying to say, and he won't admit he manipulates. He's good with words, and he's lovable and cute. Oh, God, it's happening right now. I'm confused."

"I'd really like to get some clarity here," said Tim.

I suggested that we proceed with a two-person sentence-completion exercise. Once they were seated facing each other, I said, "Take a moment before we start. Pay attention to what you're feeling right now. See if you can expand your awareness to include your partner. Can you pay attention to your own feelings at the same time that you're perceiving another human being? Or is it always one or the other? Attend to that."

Tim winked at her. Lucy siled back nervously. It was not a promising start. Locking themselves into the old pattern—manipulative on his part, conciliatory on her part—was not the best way to go about a reexamination of the relationship. I let it go by without comment.

We began working with sentence stems such as **One of the things I'd like you to know about me is—, Ever since I was a child—, I am a person who—**. These warm-ups or icebreakers relax people into the method of sentence completion, establishing a context for intimacy and beginning the process of self-disclosure in a fairly easy way.

Both Lucy's and Tim's completions reflected concern about being young, insecure, and lonely. Listening and watching them, I was struck by how much younger then her actual age Lucy seemed. Approaching her forties, she carried herself like a woman in her twenties; both her dress and her mannerisms were of a much younger woman. This and Tim's cultivated boyishness suggested an avenue to explore. Looking directly at Tim, Lucy did completions for **The bad thing about growing up is—**

I can't be a little girl anymore.

I'll have to make decisions.

I can't wait for you to make everything right.

no one will take care of me.

I'll have to take a hard look at this relationship.

I'll have to do something.

I'll be alone.

I'll never get what I wanted when I was young.

I wanted her to pay special attention to that last ending. I asked her to repeat the entire sentence three times before continuing. One of the most powerful motives for resisting growing up is the subconscious fantasy that if one remains a child, someone will come to heal the hurts and frustrations of childhood. Lucy continued:

*I'll have to accept my parents
didn't have it to give.*

I'll have to accept that you can't be a substitute.

I'll have to say good-bye to my childhood before I'm ready.

I don't know how to be an adult.

Still gazing at Tim with the wide-open eyes of a young girl, she proceeded with **The good thing about a man like you is—**

you're intelligent.

you're funny.

you're supportive, even if not all the time.

you keep me off balance.

it's exciting to be with you.

the insecurity I feel is familiar.

I've been here before.

you make me want to get from you what I never got from my mother and father.

if I can win with you, what a victory!

you're sexy.

I can't let go of you.

sometimes you drive me crazy.

The pattern emerging in Lucy's responses was one of dependency I discussed in *The Psychology of Romantic Love:*

> Many a person faces life with an attitude that, if translated into explicit speech, which it almost never is, would amount to the declaration, "When I was five years old, important needs of mine were not met—and until they are, I'm not moving on to six!" On a basic level these people are very passive, even though, on more superficial levels, they may sometimes appear active and "aggressive." At bottom, they are waiting, waiting to be rescued, waiting to be told they are good boys or good girls, waiting to be validated or confirmed by some outside source.

> So their whole lives may be organized around the desire to please, to be taken care of, or, alternatively, to control and dominate, to manipulate and *coerce* the satisfaction of their needs and wants, because they don't trust the authenticity of anyone's love or caring . . . .

> Whether their act is to be helpless and dependent, or to be controlling, overprotective, "responsible," "grown-up," there is an underlying sense of inadequacy, of nameless deficiency, that they feel only other human beings can correct. They are alien-

ated from their own internal sources of strength and support; they are alienated from their own powers . . . .

Immature persons tend to view others as sources of gratification for their own desires and needs, much as an infant views a parent. They create relationships of dependence and manipulation because they cannot see a relationship as an encounter between two autonomous human beings who are free to express themselves honestly and free to enjoy each other's independence and vitality. The immature person expects love to assuage the sense of incompleteness felt within, to quiet the fears of inadequacy, to magically finish all the unfinished business of childhood. In effect, love becomes a substitute for evolution toward maturity and self-responsibility.

When asked for her reaction to her sentence completions, Lucy acknowledged much of what is contained in the above profile of the immature personality. I had the sense that before she came to therapy, Lucy had already reached a point in her evolution where she was preparing to break free of the pattern of dependency disclosed in her sentence completions (an assumption that was later confirmed).

Now I turned my attention to Tim, suggesting that he begin with the same stem as Lucy. **The hard thing about growing up is—**

I don't want to.

I enjoy being young.

being old means being limited.

I like to keep my options open.

I like freedom.

I don't want to be confined.

I don't want to die as young as Father did.

I interrupted to ask at what age his father had died.
"Young. Sixty-two."
I gave him a new stem. **The good thing about a woman like you is—**

you're beautiful.

you're young.

you take good care of me sometimes.

we're very compatible sexually.

you admire me.

you understand me.

when you don't understand me, you accept my getting mad at you.

you can be very exciting.

you can be very funny.

you're afraid.

you relate to my fears.

we touch at some very deep level.

I was sure in the beginning that you were going to be the final woman for me.

I feel young with you.

As I sat listening, part of my mind was reviewing material Tim had presented in previous sessions. I asked him to pause, breathe deeply, go on looking at Lucy, and take a moment to focus on his feelings. Bits and pieces were coming together now. I wasn't sure yet where we were going, but I had a good idea of which direction. In an offhand tone of voice I said, "Go with the stem **At the thought that I'm going to die someday—**."

Tim flashed me a glance of astonishment, then turned back to Lucy. **At the thought that I'm going to die someday—**

I feel afraid.

I don't want it to be true.

I don't want to think about it.

it makes me sad.

I want sex.

I feel "Not me."

I want to cry.

I feel helpless.

I feel rage.

I feel it isn't fair.

When a child first learns about death—

he doesn't believe it.

he can't understand it.

he can't believe it will happen to him.

he feels betrayed.

he wants his mother.

he doesn't want his parents to leave him.

he runs away.

it's too much for him.

If talking about death weren't taboo—

I'd talk about it.

the whole subject wouldn't be so frightening.

I could admit how much time I spend being afraid of it.

I could admit how much it occupies my thoughts.

I might find out other people feel as I do.

I could be more accepting.

If I felt free to talk about my fear of death—

I might not be so afraid.

I might accept the fact of dying more readily.

I wouldn't be so tense.

my heart wouldn't be beating so fast.

I could stop running.

I could allow myself to live in the present.

I wouldn't always be wondering what I'm missing.

I think the terror would begin to go away.

something inside me would relax.

I could understand love.

One of the ways I keep myself from dying is—

I keep running after women.

I'm always dissatisfied with whatever I'm doing.

I'm always exercising and working out and thinking about staying young.

I date a lot of young women.

I never commit myself for long to one kind of work.

I don't commit.

I don't allow myself to love.

I select women I know I'll never be fully in love with.

I always tell myself this isn't it.

I pretend life really hasn't begun yet.

When working with a client who is himself a practicing psychotherapist, one needs always to be aware of the possibility of facile glibness rather than real progress. It was the look of astonishment on Tim's face as he was speaking that inclined me to feel that his involvement in the process was authentic. He had the look of a man hearing things he had never heard before, almost as if someone else were speaking. He was in an altered state. Instead of sentence completion merely being a tool that he was using, he was allowing himself to be a vehicle for the operation of sentence completion. This is the ideal way to work.

I gave him the stem **If I don't fully participate in life—**

death can't catch me.

I'll always be too young to die.

it won't be my turn yet.

I'm safe.

children don't die, only grown-ups die.

I'll die without ever having lived.

I'll throw my life away.

I'll be a coward.

I delude myself that time isn't passing.

Finally, in order to facilitate integration of what he had been saying, I proposed the stem **I'm slowly becoming aware—**

that I'm afraid of dying.

that I'm afraid to commit to anything.

no work would satisfy me with my attitude.

no woman could satisfy me.

playing around the edges of my life isn't going to keep me immortal.

I have to talk about my fear of dying.

I have to make peace with death before I can live.

there's no way a woman can win with me.

I'm afraid ever to say, "This is it."

At this point I asked Tim to pause and sit silently, meditating on the things he had been saying. His work had been so productive, so rich in content, that I was glad he had recorded it for further consideration. I asked him to bring in a typed transcript at our next session.

"Boy," he said, "I never expected this—not what we got into today. This is a complete shock."

Seeing the tears in Tim's eyes, Lucy reached out to embrace him. "This explains so much," she whispered into his ear.

It was clear that Tim was still focused on himself and Lucy was focused on Tim. For now that was probably inevitable.

At its most successful, sentence-completion work rarely requires much commentary, analysis, or interpretation from the therapist. It speaks for itself. It spoke for itself that day with Tim and Lucy. How the story would end I could not predict, but I felt certain that a dialogue would now be possible between them. (This proved to be the case.) The communication impasse had been breached. Tim and Lucy learned how to talk to each other.

These three stories illustrate some of the uses of sentence completion in psychotherapy. As this book is intended to be a primer, I am confining myself to fairly simple and straightforward uses. Still, it may be pointed out, the persons involved in our three cases did have the advantage of being guided by a psychotherapist. How can men and women work with sentence completion on their own? What are its possibilities outside psychotherapy? We are ready now to begin to answer these questions.

Sentence completion is more than a means of facilitating communication. It is a means of making explicit what had been implicit, of making conscious what had been subconscious. It is a doorway into the self.

To understand this, we must first understand how sentence completion works. Obviously, it is a powerful tool for overcoming blocks, defenses, and conscious confusion. But why?

Let us look at the method more closely. At this point we shift roles from observer to active participant.

Chapter 2

❧ ——————— ❧

Experiencing Sentence Completion

Sentence completion can be done many ways. It can be done in a group, as reported in the beginning of chapter one. It can be done as a two-person exercise, as illustrated in the vignettes. It can be done on your own without a therapist, talking to yourself in a mirror or talking into a tape recorder or, as we are going to experience here, writing in a notebook.

One principle remains the same regardless of how the exercise is set up: say or write whatever comes to mind, freely and spontaneously, without worrying about the literal truth or falsehood of any particular ending. There is always the opportunity later to assess the significance of any particular completion. When the mind seems to become blank or paralyzed, invent—say or write anything. The less thinking and rehearsing while doing the exercise, the better. Especially when writing: the greater the speed, the better.

The chief aim of the stems provided below is to give you some very simple practice with the sentence-completion method, to get a feeling for how it works. Nothing more is expected.

For each stem, please write ten completions as rapidly as you can. Proceed to the next stem as rapidly as you can. You may falter after three or four, feeling absolutely convinced that you have no more completions in you. If you persevere, you will discover that you have more to say than you initially feel. Perseverance is essential here, because it is only natural that there are barriers to be broken through, resistances to be overcome.

When you have finished with the first stem, proceed to the next as rapidly as you can. You may review your completions later, whenever you wish.

❧ Communication ❧

Communication to me means

_____

_____

_____

_____

_____

_____

_____

_____

The hard thing about intimate communication is

_____

_____

_____

_____

_____

_____

_____

_____

_____

Sometimes I withdraw from communication when

_____

_____

_____

_____

_____

_____

_____

_____

_____

❧ Self-Disclosure ❧

I am a person who

_____

_____

_____

_____

_____

_____

_____

_____

One of the things I'd like people to know about me is

_____

_____

_____

_____

_____

_____

_____

_____

_____

_____

When I try to talk about things that are important to me

_____

_____

_____

_____

_____

_____

_____

_____

_____ 43

When I try to express intimate feelings

_____

_____

_____

_____

_____

_____

_____

_____

_____

If I were more open about expressing my feelings and opinions
(Don't tell yourself this sentence is not applicable to you.)

_____

_____

_____

_____

_____

_____

_____

_____

_____

When people try to talk intimately with me, sometimes I

_____

_____

_____

_____

_____

_____

_____

_____

_____

_____ 45

❦ *Exploring Obstacles to Communication* ❧

If I weren't concerned about the listener's response

_____

_____

_____

_____

_____

_____

_____

_____

_____

Sometimes I become blocked when

_____

_____

_____

_____

_____

_____

_____

_____

_____

One of the ways I sometimes make it difficult for people to talk to me is

_____

_____

_____

_____

_____

_____

_____

We are approaching the end of the first sequence of sentence stems. By now you will almost certainly have encountered some feelings of resistance, anxiety, irritation, anger—perhaps even an impulse to throw the book away. All such feelings are quite normal for people in their initial experience with sentence completion.

You may wish to ask: Aside from familiarizing myself with the technique, what is the purpose of completing all these stems? In a sense, the purpose will be different for each reader. That is, the purpose is to be found in the particular thoughts, feelings, reactions, and realizations to which you are led. An expansion of self-awareness and self-understanding has a value in its own right, and it is also a precondition to more effective contact and communication with others.

Some readers will want to go through this entire book and fill in all the stems in three or four days. Others may wish to take a month. But you should be willing to allot at least an hour for any one work session. Two hours is preferable. Find your own natural rhythm and respect it. The most important point is to persevere. The results are worth it—for yourself as an individual and for your relationship.

❧ *Reflections* ☙

Take your time absorbing the meaning of what you have written. Pause to review what you have written so far. What feelings are evoked in you? What associations? What tentative impressions or conclusions are forming in your mind? What memories are stimulated?

_____

_____

_____

_____

Reflections

49

_____

_____

_____

_____

_____

_____

And now, one last sentence completion for this chapter:

I'm beginning to suspect

_____

_____

_____

_____

_____

_____

_____

_____

Guidelines for the Use of Sentence Completions

Almost all the exercises in this book are designed in such a way that they can be done by you alone, writing directly on the pages allotted. I advise you to do them first this way; later, they can be done with a partner or with several people, such as a family or therapy group.

When you do the sentence completions aloud, verbally, with a partner or a group, do not refer to the endings you have written in this book.

Instructions on how to use sentence completion are presented in various contexts throughout the book and are summarized here for your convenience.

When doing the sentence completions alone, writing directly in this book, try to write as rapidly and spontaneously as possible, without censorship or interfering self-criticism.

If you are doing the sentence completions aloud, to a partner or in a group, the same principle applies. Nothing you write or say is inscribed in stone.

If you get stuck, and your mind goes blank, invent—don't give up and stop.

Accept the fact that some of your completions may conflict with others. Ambivalent feelings are natural.

Accept the fact that sometimes you have to exaggerate an attitude in order to get it out at all. Don't necessarily take your statements literally.

Try to keep your completions relatively short and simple. When working aloud with a partner, face to face, do completions for at least three stems, then listen silently while your partner does completions for the same three stems. Proceed back and forth in this manner until the sequence is completed.

Study the various ways sentence completion is done in case illustrations provided throughout the book. They will deepen your understanding of the procedure and help you to appreciate its possibilities.

When you are doing the exercises in this book, alone or with others, be sure you allow time without interruption, so that attention and concentration are undivided and undistracted.

If you are doing the exercise with a partner or in a group, the rule is: No arguments or comments about anyone's sentence completions while the speaker is engaged in doing the work.

When your partner (or someone in a group) is speaking, your job is to listen silently and attentively, as empathetically as possible, without interfering or distracting responses of any kind. Such responses could sabotage the entire process.

When working with your partner, take turns doing the stems in sets of three, as indicated above, and always tape-record your work. Knowing that everything each of you says is tape-recorded allows you to defer discussion until both of you have completed all the sentence stems you want to complete during a particular session. After that, there will be time for discussion. A good way to begin the discussion is to play back and listen carefully to what each of you has said.

A family would do well to follow the same procedure as a couple: no discussion until everyone has had his or her say, and use a tape recorder.

Finally, there is one other way that an individual, a couple, or a group could use the sentence stems in this book. Each person could write out his or her own completions in private, then later, share them for discussion. Obviously, when using the written version, one does not need a tape recorder.

Now let us go a little more deeply into how and why sentence completion produces the results it does.

Chapter 3

The Sentence-Completion Method

It is easy to demonstrate that we know far more than we are aware of knowing. Given the appropriate circumstances and approach, that which is apparently unknown to a person or only implicit in his understanding can be brought into consciousness.

One of the commonest examples of this phenomenon is hypnosis. We ask an adult what he received from his parents for his fifteenth birthday, and he has no idea. When he is hypnotized, guided back to his fifteenth birthday, and asked to describe what is happening, he describes a birthday party, naming the gift he has received from his parents and even the friends who are there. When he is awakened from trance, he professes to know precisely what he received from his parents for his birthday. Subsequently, his parents confirm the information. The altered state of consciousness did not create the memory but allowed it to emerge.

Here is another example, taken from my book *Breaking Free*, of how something unknown to a person in one state of consciousness may become known in another. I am questioning Henry, a young man of twenty-four, about certain features of his life at home as a child, specifically the impression of reality created by his parents. Henry is not hypnotized, although you will see how a subtle shift in his state of consciousness is achieved in the course of our discussion.

Henry: My father didn't create the sense of a contradictory world. He was consistent—perversely consistent. He always gave me the impression that I was an imposition on him. And a disappointment.

Branden: Did he ever indicate why?

Henry: It was his whole attitude. He never explained anything. He just got the message across—nothing I

53

could do was right. It was always on his face. From the day I was born. Impatience. Irritation. Contempt.

Branden: And did that make sense to you? Did it seem fair?

Henry: No. I didn't see why I should get treated that way. Oh, is that what you mean by the sense of a crazy world?

Branden: That's part of it. What else did your father do?

Henry: He would sit for hours, sometimes, not talking, not doing anything. You wouldn't dare speak to him or ask him anything. If I made the slightest noise, the roof would fall in on me. How can you not make noise when you're four or five years old?

Branden: What about your mother? What did she project?

Henry: My mother is okay. She's very nervous. She never seemed to know what to do with me. She had her own troubles.

Branden: Such as?

Henry: She was always crying about something. She would talk to me about it. I never knew what she was talking about. I was three years old when she began making me her marriage counselor.

Branden: Are you able to say what you felt for your father when you were a little boy?

Henry: I loved him, I suppose.

Branden: Imagine you're in the house and your father hasn't come home yet. *Now you hear his footsteps. He's coming home.* What do you feel? [Note the shift of tense to facilitate the desired altered state of consciousness.]

Henry: What kind of a mood will he be in? I hope he'll be cheerful. Sometimes he is. Sometimes he's in a bad mood and he yells at me. I feel fear. I never know what to expect. I never know what will make him angry. I don't know why he has to yell so much . . . . Oh, Christ . . .

Branden: That's all right. There's nothing wrong with crying . . . . *It must be very hard, being a little boy in that kind of home.* [I maintain the present tense.]

Henry: My mother is always talking about heaven. How we'll all be happy when we go to heaven. What has that got to do with anything? Do you know what I mean?

Observe how a very simple shift in the pattern of communication between me and the client assists him in recreating some of the emotional reality of childhood.

There is another well-known technique for connecting with what we know but are not aware of. Originated early in this century by Joseph Moreno, founder of psychodrama, and later adapted by Fritz Perls, founder of gestalt therapy, the technique involves talking in fantasy to a significant person in our life, one with whom we have "unfinished business." In the Moreno version someone plays the part of the significant person; in the Perls version there is only an empty chair. The principle is the same in both: if we truly move into the spirit of the exercise, we cannot avoid shifting to an altered state of consciousness, a state in which it becomes possible to express thoughts, verbalize feelings, and experience attitudes that have been denied explicit awareness. For example, a woman in therapy speaks with apparent apathy about the death of her husband. Her eyes are dull, her voice is muted, her manner is dejected. She claims to feel nothing. The therapist asks her to imagine her husband sitting in the chair opposite her and talk to him out of her direct and immediate experience.

At first she says, "Looking at you, I feel nothing. You're gone. I don't care. I knew you would leave me. Everyone leaves me." She begins to cry. "Mommy and Daddy died and left me. Why did they do that? I always knew I would end up alone. When you came home from the doctor and told me you had cancer, that was it. I was finished right then. In that moment, it was over. I'm angry. I'm so angry at you. God damn you, why did you have to leave me, too?"

An example of a different kind may be found in my version of a well-known fantasy exercise. You imagine an encounter with a wise old person in a cave or on the top of a mountain or in some other remote place. This wise being knows the answers you desperately need after your long journey. In fantasy you ask questions, such as "Who am I that I do not yet know I am?" or "How am I standing in the way of my own growth?" or "What do I need to do to let go of the pain of the past?" You listen very carefully to the answers; sometimes they come in words, sometimes in images. And then you discuss with the therapist the marvelous and illuminating things you learned from this wise old person who resides within the self.

One of the least dramatic, and yet sometimes useful, techniques for gaining access to what we do not know became a regular part of my practice almost by accident. Many years ago I asked a client some question I was sure he could answer. It was late at night, I was feeling a little tired, and when he looked at me blankly and said he didn't know, I said as a joke, "Okay, you don't know. But *if* you knew, what *might* the answer be?" This client was rather literal-minded and had little or no sense of humor; he did not seem to recognize that fatigue had driven me into a rather feeble joke. He answered the question I originally asked. After he left the office, I remained in my chair, mildly stunned and convinced that something important had happened.

It was as if the original version of my question had evoked some kind of pressure so that he lost contact with what he knew. When I conceded that he did not know, the pressure disappeared, and when I shifted from reality into the realm of "if" and "might," he felt a freedom that gave access to the appropriate answer.

These examples can be multiplied by almost countless others, but the point has been made sufficiently for our purposes. The mind does not have a sharp division between the conscious and unconscious but rather it has a *continuum of awareness*. There are degrees of awareness ranging from focused awareness to peripheral awareness to total unawareness or unconsciousness. The stages of this continuum shade into one another like adjoining colors on the spectrum. There is no barrier between focused awareness and the unconscious, nor is the distance between these states of awareness as formidable as Freud believed. (Indeed, I view the Freudian technique of free association, in which the individual merely talks at random about whatever comes to mind—a method still favored by orthodox psychoanalyists—as just about the slowest and least efficient way of gaining access to denied, repressed, or disowned experience.)

In my work I make a distinction between an *absolute* "I don't know" and a *contextual* "I don't know." Consider again the example of hypnosis at the beginning of the chapter. If a person does not know what he received for his fifteenth birthday and is then assisted to know through a hypnotic trance, it is clear that his "I don't know" is contextual. That is, in the context of his ordinary state of awareness, he truly does not know what he received for his fifteenth birthday. A change in his state of consciousness makes it possible for him to know. On the other hand, if we ask him for the population of some small town in Africa, he would say "I don't know." No hypnotic technique could draw the correct answer from him because the correct answer does not exist in him. It is not buried on some deeper level of mind; it is not forgotten or repressed. He is ignorant of the answer in the absolute sense.

When a client says "I don't know"—"I don't know what I feel;" "I don't know whether I want to remain married;" "I don't know what I was trying to accomplish by doing that;" "I don't know what I see in her;" "I don't know whether I was molested as a child or not"—I assume until it is shown otherwise that I am confronted with a contextual "I don't know," not an absolute "I don't know."

And, among all the techniques, exercises, and processes I am familiar with, sentence completion is the most serviceable to me in the day-by-day practice of psychotherapy and marriage counseling, sentence completion has proven very useful for a wide variety of problems, and sentence completion facilitates self-awareness, self-expression, and self-healing more swiftly and efficiently than other techniques.

As I will mention again, the success of sentence completion in the context of therapy rests on the therapist's confidence and conviction that the client can do that which the client may not believe he or she can do. It is easy enough for any of us to defeat himself by saying "I can't." It is the therapist's job to know that he or she can—that we all can. One of my central purposes in writing this book is to show you that you can.

I first wrote about my use of sentence-completion technique in *The Disowned Self.* I was halfway through the writing of the book when my editor telephoned me. "Nathaniel," she asked, "in the sections where you recreate dialogue and events from therapy, how much editing of the original transcripts do you do?"

"Not much. Sometimes I clean up the grammar a little or eliminate irrelevant disgressions. I reword sentences where the original contains references that the reader wouldn't be able to make sense of. And, of course, I change details that might disclose the client's identity. Why do you ask?"

"It's those sections containing transcripts of sentence-completion work that have me a bit concerned. It all moves so swiftly; people seem to get down to their feelings and motivations so fast. Will anyone believe it? Will anyone believe it really happens that way?"

"I don't know what to say. Why don't you sit in on one of my therapy sessions and see for yourself how the method works. Then you tell me if you think I am faithfully reporting what happens."

The following week she came to one of my group therapy sessions. Needless to say, some days the work flows smoothly, other days there are difficulties and nothing seems to go right. I couldn't even be certain in advance that a problem would arise on this particular day for which sentence completion would be appropriate. As it happened, one problem after another was presented that seemed right for sentence completion and everyone's work moved with electrifying speed. The experience was gratifying for me as well as for my clients, but it was not especially unusual.

After the clients had gone, my editor smiled and shrugged. "There's nothing to be done. The way you describe it is the way it happens. But it is incredible when you think of people lying on couches year after year to gain the kinds of insights that emerge here in minutes."

The stem in a sentence-completion exercise can be used in either of two ways: (1) the individual finishes the sentence with the first (more or less) spontaneous completion that occurs to him or her, without repeating the stem provided by the psychotherapist; (2) the individual repeats the stem and keeps repeating it with a new ending each time. They are related but functionally distinct procedures. The first requires the assistance of a therapist or a teacher who sets up and adapts the program of stems before and during the process. The second procedure, which this book concerns itself with, can be learned and used effectively, within limits, outside of therapy.

For the sake of comprehensiveness, I would like to give an example of therapist-guided sentence completion from *The Disowned Self.* The client was a man of thirty-four. He was in love but kept sabotaging the relationship by returning to a meaningless affair with an old girl friend. I wanted to explore what appeared to be his fear of intimacy and commitment.

I instructed him as follows: "I will say the first part of a series of incomplete sentences. As quickly and as spontaneously as possible, you will reply with the first grammatical completion of the sentence that occurs to you. Try to avoid editing, censoring, or worrying about the rightness or appropriateness of your responses. There are no right or wrong completions. We're simply interested in the first response that occurs to you. Never mind if the responses sound foolish, illogical, ridiculous, or the exact opposite of your beliefs. I suggest that you make yourself comfortable, let your hands rest at your sides, close your eyes, take a deep breath, and let your body relax. Don't try to make anything happen. Don't try to analyze. Just let what happens happen of its own accord."

These instructions create a context, a medium in which sentence completion can act as a catalyst to produce an altered state of consciousness and a new awareness.

The client was then given a deliberately innocuous phrase, in order to test his understanding of what was wanted: "When I look at the ocean—" and he immediately responded "—I see water." Now we were ready to begin.

Therapist: When I wake up in the morning—
Client: —I wonder what I have to do today.
T: All my life—
C: —I wanted to succeed.
T: Sometimes I feel—
C: —what's it all about?
T: As a man—
C: —I sometimes don't know what that means.
T: I don't understand myself because—
       [Note: "Because" is a word I no longer use in sentence completion; it invites intellectualizing or "thinking" where I want spontaneity. Today I would probably say, "The hard thing about understanding myself is—"]
C: —I'm losing control.
T: "Control" to me means—
C: —being on top of things.
T: "Being on top of things" means—
C: —not letting my feelings overpower me.
T: Why do I always—
C: —run away. I don't run away; this is ridiculous; I don't know what I'm saying.
T: Don't try to evaluate now. Just let the responses come to you. Whenever I try—
C: —I usually succeed.
T: —I want—
C: —I want—I don't know what I want.
       [As we were temporarily stuck, I abruptly changed the subject to keep the momentum going. And in an instant it became clear why it was hard for him to know what he wanted.]
T: I can't tolerate—
C: —weakness.
T: "Weakness" to me means—
C: —giving in to my feelings.
T: If I give in to my feelings—
C: —I'll be helpless
T: Sometimes I want to cry out—
C: —I'm tired of the pressure!

T: When people look at me—
C: —let them look.
T: Why do people so often—
C: —expect things of me.
T: Right now I am feeling—
C: —anxious.
T: If I sink deeper into my anxiety—
C: —I feel something unpleasant is going to happen.
T: When I look in the mirror—
C: —I wonder: Is that me?
T: Ever since I was a child—
C: —I felt tense.
T: Sexually, I—
C: —I feel safe.
T: I feel safe because—
C: —because . . . I don't know. I feel like I'm blocking.
[Here we see why I now avoid "because." He would have been far less likely to block if I had said "the safe thing about sex is—."]
T: Never mind, let's continue. Mother was always—
C: —suffering.
T: She always seemed to expect—
C: —me to do something about it. I don't know what. I never did.
T: She never—
C: —could pull herself together. She was always leaning on me.
T: That made me feel—
C: —lousy, suffocated, inadequate.
T: And it also made me feel—
C: —angry.
T: Father was always—
C: —there. Expecting things. Looking at me.
T: He never—
C: —would explain anything.
T: He always seemed to expect—
C —me to understand everything without being told.
T: He seemed to want—
C: —me never to make a mistake.
T: When I did make a mistake—
C: —he looked at me with contempt.
T: That made me feel—
C —guilty.

T: And it also made me feel—
C: —that I must never make a mistake.
T: When I'm in bed with a woman, I feel safe because—
C: —I'm close, but there's no involvement.
T: Women to me are—
C: —emotional.
T: Men to me are—
C: —they should be strong and in control.
T: Women always seem to want—
C: —me to feel things.
T: That makes me—
C: —freeze.
T: I can remember—
C: —Mother, God damn it!
T: A woman's body—
C: —is a challenge. Am I man enough?
T: Pleasure to me is—
C: —being free.
T: "Freedom" to me means—
C: —being out of reach.
T: "Being out of reach" means—
C: —you can't get hurt that way.
T: If I ever let out my anger—
C: —God help somebody!
T: I don't dare show my anger because—
C: —I show it sometimes.
T: If I ever let it all out—
C: —I'd be wiped out.
T: I'd be wiped out because—
C: —that son-of-a-bitch would kill me!
T: When I was with father—
C: —I tried to stay cool. I tried to stay out of his way.
T: Sometimes I push my thoughts away because—
C: —I don't want to know.
T: When I think that I am my parents' child—
C: —I don't think of it.
T: Sometimes I feel guilty—
C: —because I know there's something wrong with me.
T: Sometimes I want to cry out—
C: —I'm tired!
T: The thing I'm most tired of is—
C: —I don't know.
T: Right now I'm feeling—

C: —pain . . . tension at the back of my neck.

T: If I sink deeper into the tension at the back of my neck—

C: '—I can feel how tense I am.

T: I make myself tense because—

C: —how should I know? Do I make myself tense deliberately?

T: Sometimes I push my feelings away because—

C: —I'm afraid of what I'll find.

T: If I were more emotionally open—

C: —I might feel better, but I don't believe it.

T: It's hard to be emotionally open because—

C: —I can be hurt.

T: "Being hurt" means—

C: —really needing somebody.

T: If I ever admitted I really needed another person—

C: —I need Jennifer.

T: When I admit that I need Jennifer—

C: —it feels very strange.

T: When I was first unfaithful to her—

C: —I had to prove that I didn't need her.

T: When I was driving home from her apartment last week, before I called my old girl friend—

C: —I was feeling great.

T: But later I began to feel—

C: —tense.

T: And then I began to feel—

C: —cut off from everything.

T: I cut myself off from everything because—

C: —I had to get away. I couldn't stand it.

T: I was frightened because—

C: —I'm really in love.

T: When I admit that I'm in love—

C: —the pain inside is killing me.

T: Right now I want—

C: —to cry.

T: I can remember—

[This is a very useful stem whenever the client hits a block or whenever a present problem seems to be tied to some past fear or pain.]

C: —wanting my father to love me.

T: Father—

C: —didn't love anybody.

T: Thinking of him now I feel—

C: —rage.

T: If I sink deeper into my rage I feel—
C: —hurt.
T: I want to call out to him—
C: —look at me!
T: At the thought of running away from Jennifer—
C: —I feel like I'm saying goodbye to my last chance.
T: I tense the muscles in the back of my neck in order—
C: —to stop myself from feeling anything. Jesus! That's true! [Even though my sentence stem worked in this case, today I would say, "The good thing about tensing the muscles in the back of my neck is," and it will be effective a far greater percentage of the time. "In order to," like "because," runs too great a risk of inviting intellectualizing, rationalizing, or "thinking."]
T: Right now I am feeling—
C: —I'm beginning to relax.
T: When I begin to tell Jennifer what I feel for her, I want to cry because—
C: —I've never felt it before.
T: And also because—
C: —all the pain starts coming back to me.
T: The pain began when—
C: —a long time ago.
T: I can remember—
C: —the time I wanted to sit on the arm of my father's chair.
T: Father was—
C: —impatient.
T: Right now I am feeling—
C: —better. But I don't know why.
T: The most important thing I've learned today is—
C: —I'm afraid to commit myself.
T: "Committing myself" means—
C: —letting myself really care for another person, and letting the other person know how much I care.
T: I can't do that because—
C: —it feels too threatening.
T: If I didn't always have to protect myself—
C: —I could let myself be happy. I could live.
T: Basically, I—
C: —feel unreal. Or usually, anyway. Right now, I feel real. What's happening to me?

At this point, I terminated the exercise and invited my client to discuss his reactions. Very little "interpretation" on my part was necessary. My client was able to perform the synthesis himself, especially after replaying the tape recording two or three times during the following week. One of the advantages of the method is the extent to which the material virtually speaks for itself, in a manner more convincing to the client than any therapist's "analysis."

Although there are still occasions when I use the method of sentence completion described above, I prefer the procedure in which the client keeps repeating the stem with a different ending each time: it tends to open more avenues of exploration and generally evokes a more profound level of feeling. I have accumulated several hundred stems that are now standard items in my repertoire (a good deal of experience has proven them to be the most productive most of the time), but almost always I intersperse the standard items with items improvised in response to leads or reactions of the client. A second reading of the examples of sentence completion will illustrate how my stems follow, or head back into, the direction suggested by the previous ending. The improvisation of stems will be taken up again after this preparatory exercise which I would like you to complete before continuing with the general discussion of sentence completion.

Exploring Childhood Development

One of the purposes in the following exercises, in addition to deepening our grasp of sentence completion, is to begin to understand some of the steps by which we became the person we are. The theme of parental influences is introduced here. This theme will be amplified again, later in the book.

The sentence stems offered here will evoke different feelings and responses in different readers. That is natural and inevitable.

First, the work should be done alone, here in the book. Then, if you have a partner, I advise you to go through the sequence of sentence stems again (without referring back to what you have written here) sitting face to face, each of you providing completions for three or four stems while the other listens silently and attentively. Then reverse roles, then reverse roles again, and so forth.

When working with a partner, remember to always use a tape recorder.

If a sentence stem does not seem applicable to you, please do it anyway. Allow yourself to be open. Allow yourself to be surprised.

If you were not raised by your biological mother or father, substitute the name of the most appropriate person—a stepmother or stepfather, an older brother or sister, an aunt or uncle—when "Mother" or "Father" is referred to. Don't decide that you know in advance what your responses will be. You don't. Work as fast as you can. And pay attention to the spots where your own blocks or resistances arise. You can learn a great deal about yourself.

Please do not read ahead. Complete the endings for each stem before proceeding to the next. You should note that words like "always" and "never," when used in sentence completion, are to be understood as figures of speech, not to be taken literally. Do not look back and review until you have completed the entire exercise.

❧ *Remembering Mother* ❧

Mother was always

_____

_____

_____

_____

_____

_____

_____

_____

With Mother I often felt

_____

_____

_____

_____

_____

_____

_____

_____

Mother often seemed to expect

_____

_____

_____

_____

_____

_____

_____

_____

_____ 67

What I wanted from Mother and didn't get was

_____

_____

_____

_____

_____

_____

_____

_____

Mother speaks through my voice when I tell myself

_____

_____

_____

_____

_____

_____

_____

_____

Mother gave me a view of myself as

_____

_____

_____

_____

_____

_____

_____

_____

_____

_____

This might be the place for a fairly long pause before continuing. You might wish to wait for another day. The material here is too important to be rushed through hurriedly. Take your time. Absorb what you have written. Notice the feelings it evokes. Meditate on what you can learn from this experience. Meditate on what you might have written that bears on your relationships or on the difficulties in your relationships.

What is needed here and throughout the book is freedom to write whatever occurs to you and to experience fully whatever emotions rise up in you. That is the freedom a person enjoys in the context of psychotherapy, and it is a freedom that facilitates growth. But there is absolutely no reason why that freedom should be restricted to clients in therapy. It is a freedom every human being should give himself or herself.

We change and grow not by denying and disowning who we are, but by owning and expressing who we are. I elaborate on this theme—self-acceptance and self-expression as preconditions of constructive change—in considerable detail in *The Disowned Self.*

Let me remind you that not everything you have written so far may be literally true. Remember, sometimes we need to exaggerate, to overstate our case, to say one thing and then the opposite, to try different thoughts and feelings "on for size," before we are able to experience the actual truth of our situation. To repeat: nothing you write in this book is inscribed in stone.

❧ *Reflections* ❧

This is a good moment to pause and consider such questions as: How do you feel right now? What issues or problems do you find rising to the surface of awareness? What connections or realizations are beginning to fall into place within your mind?

❧ Reflections ❧

_____

_____

_____

_____

_____

_____

_____

_____

_____

_____

_____

_____

_____

_____

_____ 71

❧ *Remembering Father* ❧

Father was always

_____

_____

_____

_____

_____

_____

_____

_____

With Father I often felt

_____

_____

_____

_____

_____

_____

_____

_____

Father often seemed to expect

_____

_____

_____

_____

_____

_____

_____

_____

_____

What I wanted from Father and didn't get was

_____

_____

_____

_____

_____

_____

_____

_____

_____

Father speaks through my voice when I tell myself

_____

_____

_____

_____

_____

_____

_____

_____

_____

Father gave me a view of myself as

_____

_____

_____

_____

_____

_____

_____

_____

_____

_____

Pause here. Take as long a rest as you need. Review your completions in this sequence.

If you feel agitated by anything you have written, feel agitated. If you feel hurt, feel hurt. If you feel angry, feel angry. But don't create a catastrophe. Just allow your feelings to be there. Be a witness to your own experience.

Don't fight yourself. Don't tell yourself, "I should feel that" or "I shouldn't feel that."

If you allow your mind to meditate on the things you have written, if you allow yourself to feel the things you are feeling, if you do not deny, disown, or otherwise give yourself a bad time, you will find that all this material has its own way of sorting itself out, often on a subconscious level.

Allow the process to continue. Trust in the integrative power of your own mind. That is, trust in your mind's ability to organize, assimilate, and absorb—at its own speed and in its own way—the material that is rising within you.

When you feel ready—and take as many rests and breaks as you need—proceed to the next set of stems. But first, use the space allotted here to record the feelings, memories, thoughts, associations, and connections that are rising in your mind right now.

❧ *Reflections* ❧

_____

_____

_____

_____

_____

❧ *Reflections* ❧

❧ *The Family Drama* ❧

One of the ways I'm still trying to win Mother's approval is

_____

_____

_____

_____

_____

_____

_____

_____

One of the ways I'm still trying to win Father's approval is

_____

_____

_____

_____

_____

_____

_____

_____

_____

_____

One of the ways I sometimes try to get back at Mother is
(You may feel dead certain this stem is inapplicable to you;
experiment with it anyway)

_____

_____

_____

_____

_____

_____

_____

_____

One of the ways I sometimes try to get back at Father is

_____

_____

_____

_____

_____

_____

_____

_____

_____

If Mother thought I was in a happy sexual relationship

_____

_____

_____

_____

_____

_____

_____

_____

_____

If Father thought I was in a happy sexual relationship

_____

_____

_____

_____

_____

_____

_____

_____

_____

_____

_____

If Mother saw me making a success of my life

_____

_____

_____

_____

_____

_____

_____

_____

_____

If Father saw me making a success of my life

_____

_____

_____

_____

_____

_____

_____

_____

_____

I'm becoming aware

_____

_____

_____

_____

_____

_____

_____

_____

_____

_____

❧ *Reflections* ❧

Pause here. Review your completions. Don't worry about conflicts or discrepancies among your answers.

Use this space to record any of your thoughts, feelings, and realizations as of this point in the work.

You may find yourself making connections that don't seem directly related to what you have just been writing. Record them anyway.

_____

_____

_____

_____

_____

_____

_____

_____

_____

_____

84 _____

❧ Reflections ❧

_____

_____

_____

_____

_____

_____

_____

_____

_____

_____

_____

_____

_____

❧ *Reflections* ❧

By now it is almost inevitable that unanswered questions and problems arising out of this material have occurred to you. Do not expect to finish with a neat and tidy package, with every issue magically resolved. That is not how sentence completion works. On a conscious and subconscious level you are providing the problem-solving center of your own mind with stimuli, with material, with data. As you continue to meditate on what you have done, integrations will begin to happen more or less spontaneously. Will they always happen to your perfect satisfaction? No. But if you persevere, you will find yourself moving forward, you will find yourself seeing more and more daylight, and you will certainly find a path to communication with your partner opening wider and wider before you.

Whenever you feel ready, proceed to the next set of stems.

❧ *Summing Up* ❧

One of the things I had to do to survive was

_____

_____

_____

_____

_____

_____

_____

_____

If it ever turns out I don't need my parents' permission to be happy

_____

_____

_____

_____

_____

_____

_____

_____

_____

If it ever turns out my survival doesn't depend on my parents' approval

_____

_____

_____

_____

_____

_____

_____

_____

_____

❧ *Moving Forward* ❧

I am becoming aware

_____

_____

_____

_____

_____

_____

_____

_____

When I feel fully ready to understand what I have been saying here

_____

_____

_____

It seems obvious that

Deeper Into The Method

When I train therapists in the use of sentence completion, I encourage them to use lists such as these verbatim, without interspersing stems improvised in response to the clients completions. With practice and experience, therapists learn to create their own stems.

In contrast to free association, sentence-completion work may be described as *directed association*. The stem is a stimulus, a springboard into the self. This is why I ask clients to repeat the stem each time: it has energizing power, renewed with each repetition. Here is an example of how a therapist might improvise a sentence stem in response to the ending of a standard stem:

Therapist:	Mother was always—
Client:	Mother was always . . . yelling at me. Mother was always . . . telling me I was stupid. Mother was always . . . putting me down. Mother was always . . . saying "Why can't you be more like your sister?"
Therapist:	When Mother compared me to my sister— *(An improvised item in response to what the client has just said.)*
Client:	When Mother compared me to my sister . . . I knew I could never compete. When Mother compared me to my sister . . . I told myself "If she's the good one, then I'll be the bad one!"

The same principle applies to a couple doing a two-person sentence-completion exercise:

Therapist:	One of the things I want from you and don't know how to ask for is—
Man to Woman:	One of the things I want from you and don't know how to ask for is . . . attention. One of the things I want from you and don't know how to ask for is . . . love. One of the things I want from you and don't know how to ask

for is . . . for things to be the way they used to be.

Therapist: Things between us began to change when—
(A stem generated in response to what the man just said.)

Man to
Woman: Things began to change when . . . Jennie was born. Things began to change when . . . you got so wrapped up in motherhood you forgot about me. Things began to change when . . . the baby always came first.

I trust it has become apparent that I stick with a stem until I sense that the endings are about to be exhausted and I stick with standard items until a suggestive ending emerges which needs to be explored in greater depth.

The idea of providing a client or subject with a series of unfinished sentences and asking him or her to complete them is not new, of course. The novelty of the technique as it has evolved in my practice consists of: (1) the specific items I have developed; (2) the method of moving back and forth between standard, predesigned items and items improvised on the spot in response to the client's replies; and (3) the utilization of a complex sequence of sentence completions, developed to meet the requirement of the immediate situation and to explore some aspect of the client's experience for as long as an hour at a time without discussion, analysis, interruption, or interpretation of any kind.

When I began experimenting with the sentence-completion technique, I regarded it primarily as an information-gathering tool. I did not foresee the value it would offer to the client as a means of achieving emotional release and expanded self-awareness. These benefits, in addition to psychological integrations originating in the client, quickly became evident. While they are not achieved equally in all cases, they are almost always achieved to some extent, sometimes on the first experience of the procedure, sometimes later.

Beth was a twenty-two-year-old woman who sought therapy because of unhappiness in her marriage. She was generally passive, withdrawn, and somewhat vague. At her first therapy session Beth was entirely silent; she rarely looked at anyone.

A few minutes before the close of her second session, she said, "I have to work." Then, in a flat, unemotional tone, she said that sometimes she was unable to recognize familiar objects for what they were, they became meaningless shapes to her, and she felt frightened.

There was a rustle of tension among the other clients at the session. I do not work with the severely disturbed in group settings, and the other clients had no experience in hearing complaints of this kind.

I saw that Beth was watching me intently for a reaction, and I chose to respond casually, saying that I could understand her fear but that her experience was not especially ominous. It struck me that her eyes were a little too watchful, her movements a little too careful. I could feel some subtle calculation, waters being tested. I explained to her and to the others, "When anxiety-provoking, unacceptable feelings emerge, people often defend themselves by cutting off from their feelings so severely that a sense of depersonalization and unreality can result."

Beth indicated that she understood, but she still felt frustrated. That was what I intended. She made her next move.

"Yes," she said, "but the thing is . . . I feel I am trapped in my present incarnation. It distusbs me very much." She waited for my reaction.

"Oh, that's interesting. Can you say more about that?"

A bit confused, Beth pressed on. "Well, I feel as if I'm trapped in my present incarnation." Again she stopped, waiting.

"Go on," I said pleasantly.

More emphatically she said, "Well, what bothers me is the thought that there is a power controlling my life, intervening, manipulating me, taking over." She had decided to raise the table stakes.

The other clients were becoming more uneasy. Some of them were wondering if we were in the presence of psychosis.

"Oh, I see," I said. "That's fine. I'd like you to try an experiment. On your feet!"

I said, "We're going to work with open-ended sentences. I will give you an open-ended sentence; you'll walk around to each person here, making eye contact and really seeing him or her. Repeat my open-ended stem and finish it any way you want, without worrying whether your ending is true or false, reasonable or unreasonable. Are you willing to do that?"

She positioned herself in front of the first person in the circle and waited for further instructions.

"Begin with **When I speak of living in my present incarnation what I really mean is—.**"

When I read over this transcript I was surprised at my daring, beginning with so direct a stem rather than building up to it with a set of easier stems. She could easily have choked up, insisting that she could not work with that stem. I was counting on my manner, full of confidence and assurance, to convey that I was asking no more than she was fully capable of doing. And she responded.

Without any hesitation whatsoever, she went from person to person. "When I speak of living in my present incarnation, what I really mean is my marriage. When I speak of living in my present incarnation, what I really mean is my whole way of life. When I speak of living in my present incarnation, what I really mean is the way I've always lived."

Her posture was subtly straightening. Her eyes were becoming more alive, and her face was becoming more animated. Her breathing was deeper.

"Now we'll go on to another item. **When I speak of being trapped in my present incarnation, what I really mean is—.**"

"When I speak of being trapped in my present incarnation, what I really mean is . . . I don't know whether or not I want to leave my husband. When I speak of being trapped in my present incarnation, what I really mean is I don't want to stay and I'm afraid to leave."

"When I speak of being controlled by a power, what I really mean is—"

"When I speak of being controlled by a power, what I really mean is . . . my own feelings of helplessness. When I speak of being controlled by a power, what I really mean is my own feelings of inadequacy. When I speak of being controlled by a power, what I really mean is I want someone to tell me what to do."

When a person is using extreme language, probably not meant literally, the clause **what I really mean is** can provoke a rapid transition to the speaker's actual intent.

Several of the other clients looked at me in shock when they heard my next sentence stem. I felt certain the risk was minimal because Beth had now entered that altered state of consciousness which comes with successful sentence completion. "Now let's try **The good thing about pretending to be crazy is—.**"

A slight, almost indiscernable convulsion went through her body. "The good thing about pretending to be crazy is I won't have to experience my own pain. The good thing about pretending to be crazy is people will know I need help. The good thing about pretending to be crazy is people will take my problems seriously. The good thing about pretending to be crazy is people will do something. The good thing about pretending to be crazy is . . . people will feel sorry for me. The good thing about pretending to be crazy is people will know I'm in trouble."

"If I couldn't pretend to be crazy—"

"If I couldn't pretend to be crazy, how would people know I

needed help? If I couldn't pretend to be crazy, people wouldn't feel sorry for me. If I couldn't pretend to be crazy, I would have to start being responsible for my own life. If I couldn't pretend to be crazy . . . I would have to start making my own choices and decisions and take the consequences."

Then Beth turned to me, grinning a little impishly. She seemed utterly relaxed, in good contact with me, with the group, and with herself.

I asked her to sit down and said to her, not casually but solemnly, "Now listen. I want you to know that I hear you. I take your fear very seriously. I take your pain very seriously. Everything you're feeling is important. I respect that. Do you understand?"

"Yes."

"Do you believe me?"

"Yes."

"Okay, it really isn't necessary for you to pretend to be crazy and scare all my friends, all your friends in the group." She began to laugh, relieved.

In a subsequent session it turned out, rather predictably, that one of the frightening feelings she was blindly seeking to defend herself against was murderous rage toward her husband.

As a very young child, Beth had learned to survive by being helpless, to manipulate others into taking care of her. Helplessness became a technique of mastery and control.

Faced with the difficulties in her marriage—or more precisely, not facing them—she went into flight from reality. Her symptoms represented a twisted and misguided struggle for self-preservation. Human beings destroy themselves every day for the sake of assuring their survival. Neurosis might almost be defined as the attempt to protect one's survival and self-esteem through self-destructive avoidance of reality.

A therapy student of mine said to me afterward that he was very worried when Beth began to speak.

"Imagine what might have happened," I replied, "if the therapist got apprehensive, fell into the trap Beth was setting and reinforced her notions of craziness. To be safe, he might recommend temporary hospitalization. In an institutional environment, Beth's strategy of survival through helplessness could easily get additional reinforcement, producing more symptoms of 'craziness.' She could end up spending years of her life in there."

"But how do you get the client to cooperate with sentence completion so beautifully?"

"You have to be absolutely convinced that the client can do it. You have to know it's possible. You have to feel it so profoundly that the client learns to feel it, too."

I hope that this story and these remarks will be remembered in the pages and exercises that follow. Remember also that many thousands of people have participated in the exercises presented in this book, and many of them began by saying, "I can't do this," "That sentence stem doesn't make any sense," "I can't relate to that," "That one doesn't fit me," "This is silly," "This is so artificial," "I can't think of anything to say."

They persevered. They found a way to complete the sentences. In doing so, they were led to places within themselves that they had not visited before, and they learned to heal wounds that had remained unhealed for years, giving voice to feelings and emotions long disowned and repressed. They learned to move from self-discovery to self-expression. They learned to communicate where before they had felt communication was impossible.

The purpose of all the foregoing is to prepare you for experimenting with sentence-completion work on your own or with your partner, starting with the exercises provided in this book and then going beyond. The more thoroughly you study, absorb, and get a feel for the sentence-completion vignettes presented in these two chapters, the more you will be able to do well with the material on your own. Since the theme of this book is the utilization of sentence completion for contact and intimacy, the balance of the book will deal principally with avenues to that end.

It is necessary to say a few words about the linguistic structure of certain key sentence stems.

You will notice that many stems begin with the phrase "one of the", as in **One of the things I'm angry about is**—; **One of the things I want from you and don't know how to ask for is**—.

Why not simply say, for example, **What I want from you and don't know how to ask for is**—? The answer is that "one of the" does not demand that any particular sentence completion be *the* answer. "One of the" allows greater latitude, greater freedom, greater spontaneity, and places less demand on the speaker for a single "right" response. Remember that the purpose of sentence completion is to make it as easy as possible to gain access to material not readily available in immediate awareness.

Suppose a couple is sitting face to face, trying to resolve a difficulty between them by using sentence completion. The man is upset and angry and professes not to know why. The wife has heard a little about sentence completion, but doesn't really understand it. She says, "Try doing sentence completions with the stem **What I'm angry** about is—." The sentence stem has too much the character of a demand.

Suppose she were to say instead, "Let's try the stem **One of the things I'm angry about is—**." The husband is now freer; no particular response has to be *the* answer. He might say, "One of the things I'm angry about is . . . how heavy the traffic was coming home today. One of the things I'm angry about is . . . the boss got on my nerves today. One of the things I'm angry about is . . . I didn't like you flirting with Charlie! One of the things I'm angry about is I didn't like Charlie flirting with you! One of the things I'm angry about is what the hell is going on between you two?" Each of them now knows that the cause of his agitation is not the traffic or his boss's mood. However, the freedom to begin by talking about those subjects makes it far easier for him to come to the real point a moment later. Sentence completion facilitates, makes easier, the process of expression and awareness.

Whenever possible, we want to minimize any connotation of demand in a sentence stem. When a person is having trouble expressing feelings, we should address the problem, not attack it. **If I were willing to be vulnerable, I would tell you—; If I knew you wouldn't laugh at me, I would tell you—; If I could be certain you wouldn't hurt me—**. Allowing him or her to say "if" moves the individual from reality into fantasy, where constraints and limitations are diminished, and thoughts flow more freely and easily.

When inquiring into the reasons for some feeling or behavior, we avoid "why", "reason," "because," "in order to," and so forth. All such words risk evoking an intellectualizing process, a careful search for an explanation. We want spontaneity; we want to make it possible for the individual to leap over his or her blocks and defenses. We don't want to activate those blocks and defenses. If a man wants to explore his fear of emotional closeness, we don't propose the stem **I'm afraid of emotional closeness because—**. Instead we suggest **The bad thing about emotional closeness is —**. Or, more indirectly still, **If I were to allow you to get close to me—**.

Suppose a wife is continually late and keeps her husband waiting when they have made plans to go out. They decide to work on the problem through sentence completion. We would not suggest the stem **I keep you waiting because—**. Chances are she will insist she does not know why she is late or that there is no reason, it just happens. Instead we would suggest a stem such as **The good thing about keeping you waiting is—**, or **The payoff for keeping you waiting is—**, or **If I were always to be ready on time—**, or all three stems in sequence. She may very well protest, "There is no good

thing about keeping my husband waiting," or "There is no payoff."
Fine, granted there is nothing good about it and there is no payoff;
just the same, do the exercises and experiment. Do it as a game;
invent if you get stuck; play with it. But do it. If she is willing to
cooperate, she will quickly enough come to the reasons for her con-
tinual lateness. Just to cover all bases, it would be advisable for her to
experiment with **The bad thing about being on time is**— or **The bad
thing about not keeping you waiting is**—. Approaching a problem
from the opposite side will often provide additional insights.

Expressions such as "The good thing about" or "The bad thing
about" or "The payoff for" all aim at disclosing the goals or purposes
of behavior, sometimes at a very profound level.

*The good thing about not having an orgasm is it makes you feel inade-
quate.*

*The good thing about not having an orgasm is I can remain Daddy's little
girl.*

The bad thing about letting you close to me is you might hurt me.

*The bad thing about letting you close to me is you might not like what
you see.*

The payoff for being withdrawn is you give me a lot of attention.

The payoff for being withdrawn is I get back at you for hurting me.

When a person complains about some behavior, such as his or
her procrastination, or avoiding intimacy with a spouse, or even
feeling insecure and self-doubting, that person may be surprised and
even dismayed when asked to complete *The good thing about*— or *The
payoff for*— in connection with behavior that he or she just identified
as a problem. Here it is important to remember one of the basic rules
of sentence-completion work: Never worry about whether a particular stem seems to fit or seems applicable; experiment with it, explore
it, play with it. Find out what happens. If nothing happens, it has cost
you only a few seconds. Very often something does happen. No
matter how much I assure you beforehand, you will still be surprised
by the consistency with which apparently inapplicable stems produce
endings that you will want to follow up.

Not uncommonly the stem **If I didn't have to worry about my
image**— provokes the instant response that the individual doesn't
worry about his or her image. I routinely answer, "Fine. Do it anyway.
Just invent endings. No one is holding you accountable." And then

the person will say something like: "If I didn't have to worry about my image, I could be more relaxed. If I didn't have to worry about my image, I could be more playful with my children. If I didn't have to worry about my image, I could let my wife know when I was upset. If I didn't have to worry about my image, I could let my wife know how much I love her."

Afterward I say, "Any of those sentences true?"

"Some."

"Which ones?"

Usually the answer is, "They're all true."

Sometimes, of course, not all the endings will be true; that is acceptable, even desirable. *The freedom to say things that aren't true reinforces the freedom to say things that are true.* That is one of the basic ideas behind sentence completion.

We want to keep our stems as short and as simple and as easy to say as possible. Generally we want to keep our endings reasonably short, too. We don't want to start ending in paragraphs because we lose momentum. The piling up of too many words eventually becomes an explanation, and explanations eventually become defenses.

Let us suppose that a person or a couple, after working with sentence completion for some time, now wish to pull together and integrate the underlying meanings of what has been said. At this point we introduce a variety of "integrative" stems, stems which draw upon implicit meanings for explicit statements. These stems allow subconscious understandings to find their way into articulate speech. Such stems include:

I am becoming aware—

I am beginning to suspect—

I am beginning to see—

I am beginning to realize—

If any of what I have been saying is true—

When I am ready to understand what I have been saying—

When I am ready to accept what I have been learning—

When I am ready to see what I see and know what I know—

Usually two or three of these stems suffice in one encounter. Notice that all of them have guiding implications built into their wording. To say, for example, "I am beginning to see" or "I am beginning to suspect" is to imply: (1) I am indeed beginning to see or suspect something, and (2) there is something there for me to begin to see or suspect. "When I am ready to understand what I have been saying" contains three implicit assumptions: (1) there is no demand that I understand it right now if I do not feel ready, (2) a time will come when I will be ready, and (3) when that time comes something of consequence will follow.

When I observe that an individual is expressing important material but also fighting his or her own process, I introduce a touch of humor: **"It is slowly and reluctantly dawning on me that—."** Typically, the person smiles or laughs and then responds.

This is the spirit I hope you will bring to the exercises in this book.

I suggest you pause here, take some time to go back over the material you have written, reflect on the thoughts and feelings that are coming up for you at this point. It is natural and inevitable that unanswered questions will have arisen. You may be experiencing some puzzling feelings and emotions. You may also have been struck by now by some important insights. Give yourself credit for the distance you have already traveled, and be curious about the learnings that will come to your conscious mind at the appropriate time in the near future.

Reflections

❧ Reflections ❧

Facilitating Intimate Communication

Intimate communication is not always easy. Some of the reasons why it is difficult, even for people in love, are discussed in *The Romantic Love Question & Answer Book:*

If I am confused about my thoughts and feelings, if I am unclear as to what I am experiencing or what I want my partner to know, then I cannot express myself well.

When the simple fact of my being overwhelmed by my emotions causes difficulty in communications, I need to describe my feelings at length rather than try to race past them. Otherwise, I may become not only unclear but incoherent.

The first step toward a solution in such a case is to acknowledge my confusion and not to pretend to clarity. I can say to my partner, "I know that I am not too clear right now. Please be patient with me while I try, as best I can, to describe what I'm aware of and let's see where that might lead."

If, beyond that simple confusion, I am out of touch with my emotions, denying my needs and wants, and if I attempt to communicate without setting forth honestly what I am experiencing internally, I cannot possibly express anything that will satisfy you or me. Very likely I will go off on a tangent leaving both of us feeling helpless, bewildered, and frustrated. Back up, take a deep breath; let's try to describe the experience as we are conscious of it without intellectualizing or psychologizing, asking our partner for the right to think aloud without having to defend or justify each and every sentence. This is a freedom that wise lovers give each other.

If I am afraid of how you will respond, afraid that you won't understand and that you will be hurt or resentful, my mind may jam up when I begin to speak. I may say everything except what I most need to say, which is that I have these fears, whether well-founded or not. So our effort at communication may lead straight to estrangement.

Whenever we feel the presence of such a fear, we should be able to say to our partner, "There are things I feel the need to tell you, thoughts and feelings I want to share with you, and I am aware of my anxiety about your reaction. My fantasies of your exploding at me are inhibiting my ability to express myself."

Acknowledging our fear accomplishes two things. First, it allows us to relax a little, since we don't have to pretend about what we are feeling. Second, it increases the probability that our partner will listen acceptingly to whatever we are struggling to express, because we are trusting our partner.

Sometimes the accumulation of grievances interrupts my present train of thought. I try to stick to the point but I feel myself pulled into the past. From my partner's point of view, I am cluttering up our discussion with references to incidents long ago that don't bear in any obvious way on the present. So I need to make a further decision: Either confine myself to the present or acknowledge to my partner my need to talk about incidents that are past but still powerfully relevant to me. Again, it is very helpful to describe my state to my partner and ask for a genuine effort at understanding.

It takes time. Communication can break down because I feel I do not have enough time to explain. I may have been preparing to discuss some important matter with my partner when he or she says, "Okay, we have half an hour. What's on your mind?" The clock is like a gun aimed at my head; I cannot think. Therefore, I cannot speak effectively. Rather than try, it is far better to describe my feelings and ask for another time when we can speak at greater leisure.

Obviously, none of the difficulties we are describing here is confined to people in love. If they appear to come up most frequently in love relationships, it is because, as we have already indicated, we are most likely to be speaking from deep emotions in such relationships. Fears and blocks are that much more likely to sabotage our efforts.

If I see that my partner is struggling to tell me something and the message isn't getting through, often I can be helpful by saying, "Stop. Take a deep breath. Forget about the subject under discussion. Just describe to me what you're feeling right now in as much detail as you can." We have found that such an approach has an almost magical power between two people who love each other, even when they feel cut off.

All these considerations need to be kept in mind when doing sentence completion. The person doing the completions must feel free to say *anything*. In a two-person exercise, the job of the listener is to be there openly and receptively without answering, without rebuking, without becoming defensive, facilitating rather than obstructing. If my partner does not feel that I will give him or her a respectful, attentive hearing, how can I hope for honest, clear, or straightforward communication?

This question might arise: Isn't it possible that sentence completion may lead an individual or a couple into material too complex, or even too devastating, for them to deal with? My experience tells me that the answer is no. Troublesome revelations occur, undeniably. If a couple does not panic or give up, persevering with the methods described in this book, the chances are very high they will find their way to a resolution. Every crisis, it is useful to remember, is an opportunity for growth. An excessive fear of "rocking the boat" does not serve relationships so much as it tends to subvert them. In some cases, a couple may be led to realize that they do indeed need outside professional assistance and should not hesitate to seek it. Or, less desirable but sometimes inevitable, they may decide by tacit agreement to "forget about" the items they don't know how to handle.

If a couple decides to attempt intimate communication, they cannot know in advance everything that might be said and precisely where their efforts might lead them. Some risk is inherent in any attempt at honest communication, but risk is scarcely an argument against the attempt. Few psychotherapists or marriage counselors would dispute that for every relationship wrecked because of what someone said, a thousand are wrecked because of what someone failed to say. Silence, not speech, is the enemy of romantic love. I might add that a great deal of assistance in handling the kinds of issues that might arise in the exercises may be found in *The Romantic Love Question & Answer Book* and *The Psychology of Romantic Love*.

Not everyone can afford to go to a psychotherapist or a marriage counselor, and competent ones can be hard to find. Men and women need tools they can use on their own. The contemporary concern with self-help is not a fad, but an urgent practical necessity if human beings are to create happier lives for themselves. Qualified psychologists need to make themselves responsible for the quality of the self-help programs offered.

In the chapters that follow, we shall look at various aspects of relationships, at the kinds of communication impasses that can arise, at the kinds of problems couples have difficulty talking about, and at the solutions sentence completion can generate. We shall touch briefly on how sentence-completion techniques can be used in families.

I would like to conclude this chapter with an exercise that can be done by an individual, by a couple, or by an entire family (or, for that matter, a group in the context of therapy).

A Self-Sharing Exercise

Begin by completing the sentence stems listed in the following pages in private, as rapidly as you can. If more than one person is participating, each person should first do the exercise on his own, each person using a separate notebook.

❧ Self-Sharing ❧

All my life

_____

_____

_____

_____

_____

_____

_____

_____

_____

One of the things I wish people (you, my partner) understood about me is

_____

_____

_____

_____

_____

_____

_____

_____

_____

If the child in me could speak, he/she might say

_____

_____

_____

_____

_____

_____

_____

_____

_____

It isn't easy for me to admit

_____

_____

_____

_____

_____

_____

_____

_____

_____

If I were willing to be vulnerable

_____

_____

_____

_____

_____

_____

_____

_____

_____

_____

_____

If I could be certain I wouldn't be laughed at

_____

_____

_____

_____

_____

_____

_____

_____

If I could be certain I wouldn't be condemned

_____

_____

_____

_____

_____

_____

_____

_____

If I could admit how lonely I sometimes feel

_____

_____

_____

_____

_____

112 _____

Aloneness to me means

While every reader is encouraged to proceed at his or her own natural rhythm, this seems like a good place to take a rest and a break, to reflect on what you have written. Explore your feelings, practice accepting whatever you are feeling right now without trying to change it, and allow the subconscious as well as the conscious level of mind to process and assimilate the material that has become available to this point.

A few notes on your reactions might be helpful here.

◀ *Reflections* ▶

_____

_____

_____

_____

_____

_____

_____

_____

_____

_____

❧ Reflections ❧

Assumptions About Masculinity, Femininity, Marriage, Sexuality

A man to me means

_____

_____

_____

_____

_____

_____

_____

_____

_____

_____

A woman to me means

_____

_____

_____

_____

_____

_____

_____

_____

_____

Marriage to me means

_____

_____

_____

_____

_____

_____

_____

_____

_____ 117

Emotional security to me means

_____

_____

_____

_____

_____

_____

_____

_____

_____

If I didn't have to worry about my image

_____

_____

_____

_____

_____

_____

_____

_____

_____

_____

If I could admit that sometimes I'm delicate

_____

_____

_____

_____

_____

_____

_____

_____

_____

If I could admit how much anger I have locked up inside of me

_____

_____

_____

_____

_____

_____

_____

_____

If I could admit how much love I have locked up inside of me

_____

_____

_____

_____

_____

_____

_____

_____

_____

_____

_____

Sometimes I feel frustrated when

_____

_____

_____

_____

_____

_____

_____

_____

_____

If I felt free to show people (or my partner) my excitement

_____

_____

_____

_____

_____

_____

_____

And now, "primed" by the preceding, do completions for the following stems.

I can remember

_____

_____

_____

_____

_____

_____

_____

_____

_____

_____

If I were willing to breathe deeply and feel the energy inside of me

_____

_____

_____

_____

_____

_____

_____

_____

Working With A Partner Or In A Group

Once you have done this exercise alone, you will be ready to appreciate the expanded possibilities in sentence completion as a two-person technique. In the two-person exercise, one of you agrees to begin in the role of listener, the other in the role of speaker: you listen to your partner's ten completions for several stems; then you reverse roles and you work with the same stems; then you reverse again for several more stems; and so on.

Do not refer to your written answers when doing the completions with a partner. Chances are good that some new and different endings will occur to you. Remember, do the exercise with a tape recorder so that you and your partner can later play back what each of you has said. Take time to discuss your feelings, reactions, and thoughts.

When this exercise is done with a family or a group, the rules and procedures are first explained by a leader who has read and mastered the material here. The leader calls out the first stem, and each person in the circle (including the leader) repeats the stem and adds an ending. (In the case of therapy groups, the therapist may or may not choose to participate with endings.) The group goes around with the same stem from six to ten times. The leader says "Pause," and introduces the next stem.

It can hardly be overemphasized that in order for sentence completion to be successful an atmosphere must be created in which each participant feels free to say whatever comes to mind without fear of recrimination or attack. You don't have to agree with everything said, but everyone's feelings must be acknowledged and respected.

In sentence-completion work, as in any form of communication, the importance of effective listening must be stressed. The right kind of listening facilitates communication just as the wrong kind obstructs it. This issue is elaborated on in considerable detail in *The Romantic Love Question & Answer Book* and also in *The Psychology of Romantic Love*.

I can listen in a way that communicates I am genuinely interested, and I can listen in a way that conveys I am acting out of duty with no genuine involvement. I can listen in a way that makes communication easier for my partner—or harder.

If my eyes are looking off in some other direction while my

THE SENTENCE-
COMPLETION
METHOD

partner is attempting to pour out his or her heart to me, I am obstructing communication rather than facilitating it. If I am listening with a tense expectancy that conveys that I am more interested in offering my rebuttal than in understanding what is being said, then I am sabotaging communication again.

If, on the other hand, I am willing to listen openly, nondefensively, with a genuine wish to give my partner the experience of being heard, then I am supporting communication and the resolving of whatever pain or conflicts exist between us.

To quote from *The Psychology of Romantic Love:*

What we want from our partner is interest, the desire and willingness to listen. We want our emotions to be taken seriously, to be respected. We do not wish to be told, 'You shouldn't feel that.' Or 'It's foolish to feel that.' We do not wish to be lectured. Very often the healing is achieved, or the solution is found, through the simple act of expressing our pain. Nothing more is needed. We want our partner to understand that. And our partner needs the same understanding from us. When each can give this understanding to the other, the bond of love is strengthened. . . .

The greatest gift we can sometimes give a person we love is just to listen, just to be there, just to be available, without any obligation to say something brilliant, or to find a solution, or to cheer our partner up. But to be able to give that to another, we must be able to give it to ourselves. If we are harsh and moralistically judgmental toward ourself, we will not treat our partner any better. Self-acceptance is the foundation of acceptance of others. The acceptance of our own feelings is the foundation of our acceptance of the feelings of others. . . .

If we wish to be in a love relationship, we owe to our partner the freedom for him or her to express anger. We owe it to our partner to listen, not to interrupt, not to fight back, but to listen. After our partner is finished, after he or she feels satisfied about having said everything, then and then only is it appropriate to respond. Then, if we believe our partner has misinterpreted the facts, we can point that out. If it is clear that we are in the wrong, the solution is to acknowledge that. . . .

We need to ask ourselves: Can I accept my partner's expressions of love? Of joy? Of excitement? Can I allow my partner to feel, to experience, and to convey such states, whether or not I am always fully able to share them? Or do I turn my partner off, as others once turned me off, as, perhaps, I have learned to turn myself off.

Small wonder that people who cannot handle the realm of emotion—either happy emotions or unhappy ones—complain that inevitably 'passion dies.' The miracle, perhaps, is not that for them passion dies but that passion ever existed at all, even for a moment. That it can and does is a tribute to the power of the life force within us, which, breaking through the barrier of our repression and self-alienation, however briefly, points the way to the possibility of ecstasy. Our task is to learn not to betray that possibility.

In my therapy sessions sometimes I invite the client or the group to work with the stem **The bad thing about you (Nathaniel) is—**. I remain silent while the individual or the group works with this stem until the full range of negative feelings has been aired. I do this for several reasons. First, I believe it is fully natural that clients will at times have negative feelings toward a therapist, and expression of these feelings should be allowed and encouraged. Second, the therapist can gain valuable insights to improve the quality of his work. Third, such an exercise is a convincing demonstration that nothing is forbidden to be said. There are no authority figures whom one dare not criticize. I have received a lot of valuable feedback in this way, feedback that has helped me both as a therapist and as a human being.

I was very impressed by an enterprising client many years ago who, after seeing this exercise done, taught it to her eight-year-old daughter. As they sat in chairs facing each other, she encouraged her little girl to do completions with the stem **The bad thing about you, Mommy, is—**. At first the daughter was suspicious; she could scarcely believe she was going to be allowed to air her grievances without punishment or retaliation. When she saw that her mother was sincere, that her mother really wanted to know, that her mother was genuinely open and receptive, the result was a transformation of their relationship. They became closer and far more loving than they ever had before.

I was thrilled when she reported this experience to the group. "Just imagine what it would be like," I said to the group, "to be raised in a home where mothers and fathers invited us to do sentence completions beginning with **The bad thing about you, Mother, is—** and **The bad thing about you, Father, is—**. Had you all been reared in such homes, I doubt that I would have had the pleasure of meeting any of you."

The bad thing about you is not a sentence stem I would ordinarily recommend between two adults. Used in relation to a therapist, the stem involves a bit of irony or even humor. In the case of a child speaking to an adult, the stem is usually not offensive or threatening. With adults, however, it is better to say, **One of the things I resent about you is—.**

I am aware of the fact that if you have completed all the exercises to this point, you probably feel bombarded with more material than you can assimilate. Such a feeling is entirely natural and normal. It is no cause for concern. Right now, as you are reading these words, other levels of your mind are working on processing and assimilating what has come to you thus far. The mind's inherent thrust is toward integration. Not all of the integration needs to occur at an explicit and conscious level.

If there are some feelings of agitation, do your best to accept them without drawing catastrophic conclusions. A great deal may be stirred up in you by now. You are on a journey and an adventure and, like any important adventure, some element of anxiety is an inherent part of the process. And would adventure be as enticing without it?

❧ Reflections ❧

Please take some time now for any reflections on where this book has brought you mentally and emotionally.

_____

_____

_____

_____

_____

_____

_____

_____

_____

_____

_____

_____

_____

❧ Reflections ❧

❧ Reflections ❧

Chapter 4

Understanding And Expressing Feelings—1

The stems in this chapter and the next aim at enhancing emotional self-awareness: what triggers certain key emotions, and what behaviors follow as a result. This paves the way for the possibility of change in how we feel and what we do about how we feel.

A major purpose of this book is to demonstrate the extent to which sentence completion can disclose unrecognized attitudes and patterns. By doing the exercises that follow, your self-awareness—and consequently, your ability to communicate—will grow. That is the one prediction I will make at this point.

Please allow yourself enough time for the process to happen. The sentence stems are progressively organized so that best results will be achieved by working through a chapter at a time. Reserve a full afternoon or evening, free of all interruptions, for each chapter. You will find that the present topic, exploring your adult emotional life, takes at least that long.

Your completions should be written in the space provided in this book. Later, using a tape recorder rather than a notebook, you can work with the same stems with a partner or a friend in a two-person exercise. First, one person does completions for a set of stems while the other listens quietly and attentively, then the roles are reversed, then reversed again as they continue to new stems. The open-ended sentences I provide can be used between couples, friends, or with an entire family or therapy group, in the manner described earlier.

But let us begin the work as a private enterprise for you alone.

You will have encountered a few of these stems before. The repetitions are deliberate. Take a moment to relax; breathe deeply. Do your best to turn your mind on automatic pilot, and go!

❧ *Hurt* ❧

Sometimes I feel hurt when

_____

_____

_____

_____

_____

_____

_____

_____

_____

Sometimes when I'm hurt, I

_____

_____

_____

_____

_____

_____

_____

_____

_____

One of the ways I sometimes hide my hurt is

_____

_____

_____

_____

_____

_____

_____

_____

_____

One of the ways my hurt comes out is

_____

_____

_____

_____

_____

_____

_____

_____

If I ever fully admitted when I feel hurt

_____

_____

_____

_____

_____

_____

_____

_____

_____

_____

_____

A better way to deal with my hurt might be

_____

_____

_____

_____

_____

_____

_____

_____

_____ 135

❧ *Reflections* ❧

Pause here and review your completions. Try not to draw too many conclusions at this point. Just observe what you have written and record the thoughts, associations, and conclusions that have occurred to you so far.

_____

_____

_____

_____

_____

_____

_____

_____

_____

_____

_____

_____

❧ *Reflections* ❧

❧ Fear ❧

Sometimes I feel afraid when

_____

_____

_____

_____

_____

_____

_____

_____

Sometimes when I'm afraid, I

_____

_____

_____

_____

_____

_____

_____

_____

_____

One of the ways I sometimes hide my fear is

_____

_____

_____

_____

_____

_____

_____

_____ 139

_____

One of the ways my fear comes out is

_____

_____

_____

_____

_____

_____

_____

_____

_____

If I ever fully admitted when I feel afraid

_____

_____

_____

_____

_____

_____

_____

_____

_____

_____

_____

A better way to deal with my fear might be

_____

_____

_____

_____

_____

_____

_____

_____

_____ 141

❧ *Reflections* ❧

Again, try not to draw premature conclusions. After you have meditated on what you have written, without attempting to judge it, pause for a while to record your reactions and reflections.

_____

_____

_____

_____

_____

_____

_____

_____

_____

_____

_____

_____

❧ Reflections ❧

❧ Feeling Threatened ❧

Sometimes I feel threatened when

_____

_____

_____

_____

_____

_____

_____

_____

Sometimes when I feel threatened, I

_____

_____

_____

If I were willing to look clearly at the things that threaten me

❧ *Anger* ❧

Sometimes I feel angry when

_____

_____

_____

_____

_____

_____

_____

_____

_____

Sometimes when I'm angry, I

_____

_____

_____

_____

_____

_____

_____

_____

_____

One of the ways I sometimes hide my anger is

_____

_____

_____

_____

_____

_____

_____

_____

_____ 147

One of the ways my anger comes out is

_____

_____

_____

_____

_____

_____

_____

_____

_____

If I ever fully admitted when I feel angry

_____

_____

_____

_____

_____

_____

_____

_____

_____

_____

A better way to deal with my anger might be

_____

_____

_____

_____

_____

_____

_____

✧ *Reflections* ✧

Take this opportunity to record whatever impressions or conclusions are rising in your mind at this time. You have traveled a long way and you have a long way yet to go. But this is a good point for a pause, a review of where you have been, a summary of what is developing inside of you thus far, especially any sense of what you are learning.

_____

_____

_____

_____

_____

_____

_____

_____

_____

_____

❧ *Reflections* ❧

❧ Reflections ❧

Let me remind you that you may wish to go back to various sections in this chapter or the preceding chapters and add additional completions to those you have already entered for various sentence stems. And you may wish to add additional notations concerning your thoughts and reflections.

You may even wish to keep a separate notebook so that you can work further with the sentence stems offered throughout this book—an ongoing journal that you can continue more or less indefinitely. One of the many values of doing so is that you may discover that certain themes keep recurring while others assume less importance as time goes by. You will certainly discover that certain problems seem to resolve themselves.

Work of this kind takes courage. Failure of nerve can cause you to let go of this project permaturely. I am aware that the sentence stems I am providing are bombarding you with stimuli. I am also aware that if you follow this project through to the end, you will be led to a great many resolutions and clarifications.

This is not to say that every question will be answered and every problem resolved. Any such promise would be absurd. The case illustrations I relate throughout this book are intended to act as guides, to make real the kind of breakthroughs that are possible, to illuminate some of the dangers you will have to confront, and to dramatize the value of persevering.

We can now examine (without biasing your completions) how some of the preceding stems might be adapted to resolve a specific problem.

Sarah began a therapy session by saying, "Last week Harry and I got into two arguments, both of which I started. After they were resolved, it turned out I thought I was angry about one thing when I was really angry about something else. I do that a lot. I would like some suggestions on how to figure out what's really making me angry.

"We had the first argument when Harry came home late from work. He told me he would be late, but I had forgotten. I know now I was angry because he didn't show any sympathy about how worried I had been. I didn't even mention it when he came in. Five minutes later, something came up about cleaning the kitchen, and I got mad all out of proportion to that problem."

I asked, "How would you like things to be?"

"I would like to know, first of all, when I'm upset and what I'm upset about. I'm getting better at knowing when I'm upset, but I still don't always know what I'm upset about. And I'd like to know how to respond better."

Sarah's question—What am I really angry about?—can only be answered by the person who is angry, with or without the aid of a psychotherapist. Allowing the answer to emerge is often a matter of not pressing for it, not trying to crash through the mental block, but rather clearing a path along which the answer can travel.

Drawing from the group of stems you have just covered, I asked Sarah to complete some sentences. She began with **Sometimes I get upset when Harry—**

gets home late.

forgets to put the laundry away.

thinks I'm okay when I'm not okay.

thinks I'm not okay when I am okay.

makes me do something I don't want to do.

promises to do something and doesn't do it.

I feel hurt when Harry—

leaves me out.

is busy, and I can't be involved.

doesn't appreciate my feelings.

goes somewhere with me, and he doesn't want to go there.

doesn't understand how I feel about things.

doesn't include me in what is going on in his life.

One of the ways I deny my hurt is—

by thinking about something else.

by thinking something good about myself.

by concentrating on something wrong with Harry.

by thinking about something I've been bothered by and thinking about it and thinking about it and thinking about it—without really thinking.

UNDERSTANDING
AND EXPRESSING
FEELINGS—1

The bad thing about knowing when I'm hurt is—

I might be hurt more than I think.

if I know when I'm hurt, I have to tell Harry about it and maybe he won't like me.

I have to tell Harry about it, and then he'll know how weak I am.

I don't want to be weak.

I shouldn't ever be hurt.

If Harry ever finds out he has the power to hurt me—

he'll leave me.

I interjected, "Say that again, please." She did so, then continued:

he'll know something about me I don't want him to know.

he'll hurt me more.

I'll react by hurting him.

he'll be more careful.

maybe he'll find out he has some other powers, too.

Sometimes I get angry when Harry—

gets home late.

forgets something that's important to me.

makes light of something that's important to me.

expects too much of me.

is abrupt with me.

doesn't get involved with things I think are important.

The bad thing about telling Harry when I'm angry is—

he might hate me for it.

I don't want him to think I'm a shrew.

he might think that I'm angry all the time and I'm just not telling him.

he might turn to someone else who's not angry.

he might get angry back.

If I could be certain Harry would accept my anger—

I could love him more.

then I could be certain that he loves me.

then I'd feel more secure.

then we'd always know where we stood.

Mother used to make me think—

that it was wrong to get angry.

that anger was childish.

if I got angry I was bad.

anger is evil.

If it turns out that Harry is not my mother—

I'm going to be so relieved!

then maybe I can be more real to him than I was to her.

then I'm going to be able to be completely visible to somebody.

I'll be able to show who I really am.

I'll find out what I'm really like, too.

then I'm going to be a lot happier.

then who is he?

then I hope he isn't my father.

Father used to make me think—

that little girls don't get angry.

mature people that he respected didn't get angry.

adults don't get angry.

that anger was something to be disapproved of.

If it turns out that Harry is neither my mother nor my father—

then I'm going to have to reevaluate my relationship to Harry.

maybe I'll be able to communicate better with him than I do with them.

I'll be happier.

I'm going to have to redefine our whole relationship.

maybe it'll be okay to be who I am with him.

then maybe I can get angry and enjoy it.

maybe he can accept my anger and enjoy the fact that I'm able to express it.

If Harry were to hear the things I've been saying here—

he'd say, "Of course."

he'd say, "I didn't know you thought I was like your father."

he'd understand me a little better.

he'd be happy for me.

If I were willing to let him see this side of me—

I'd be a lot happier.

he'd be a lot happier.

we'd know where we stood all the time, and that would sure be nice.

then my relationship with him would go the direction I want it to go.

I'd be closer to him than I would be to my parents.

If I were to be closer to Harry than to my parents—

that would be scary because I'd be cutting off my parents.

it would be a kind of growing up that I'm not sure I want to do.

then it would be risky because what if Harry leaves me? Parents never leave you.

my parents would be jealous, and they'd make a fuss, and I'd have to do something about it.

my parents would figure it out, and they wouldn't be very happy.

If I had my parents' permission to love Harry fully—

then they wouldn't be my parents.

what do I need their permission for, anyway?

If it ever turns out that I could love a man without my parents' permission—

I'll be surprised.

maybe I'll be able to move away with my husband and live somewhere else and not feel guilty about it.

I'll be a lot happier.

my parents are going to be unhappy.

then the man will probably be Harry.

then I'm not going to see so much of my parents.

I'm beginning to suspect—

my relationship with Harry would deepen if I could cut the ties with my parents.

I should have outgrown this a long time ago.

if I could express myself to Harry, I would be closer to him.

I'm afraid I'd be lost without my parents.

I am going to make a better relationship with Harry if I can only be more open with him.

anger is one of the things I was never allowed to express when I was a kid.

I don't know how to express anger.

I'm afraid to try.

I'm afraid of what might happen if I expressed anger.

I've never seen much of anyone getting angry.

if I express my anger more, I'd feel happier.

"Lots to think about," I said to her.

"Thank you."

In subsequent sessions we explored Sarah's association of abandonment and loss of love with expressions of anger. She was coached to use appropriate self-expression and self-assertiveness with her husband Harry and with people generally. Sarah tape-recorded all her sentence-completion work, a practice I encourage as a matter of routine. Harry had the opportunity to listen to the tape, which paid a dividend in Harry's better understanding of her fears and in his support throughout her struggle toward greater emotional honesty.

Take a moment to consider whether any aspect of Sarah's and Harry's story might pertain to you and your partner's relationship. Space is included here for any thoughts and reflections you may wish to record.

❧ Reflections ❧

❧ *Reflections* ❧

After going through the stems in this chapter individually, partners or friends can do them together as a two-person exercise. Or the stems can be used in a family or group therapy setting.

Always follow the sequence of stems as presented here in the book, but allow yourself time to take rests when needed. This is work.

Remember, no one comments on or discusses anyone else's endings while the work is in process. Everyone listens respectfully and attentively. A context of acceptance and freedom is essential for success.

Here are some additional stems that couples find useful:

One of the ways I sometimes hurt you is—

One of the ways I sometimes make you angry is—

One of the ways I sometimes frustrate you is—

One of the ways I sometimes make it difficult for you to love me is—

One of the ways I sometimes make it difficult for you to give me what I want is—

Individuals or couples who have done the stems presented so far will almost inevitably have acquired a feel for the method. From this point on, it should become increasingly possible to improvise stems to meet specific situations.

Suppose someone says, "One of the ways I make it difficult for you to give me what I want is I don't tell you what I want. One of the ways I make it difficult for you to give me what I want is I pretend I don't want anything. One of the ways I make it difficult for you to give me what I want is I reject whatever you offer." In such a case, a natural follow-up stem might be **The bad thing about allowing you to give me what I want is—** or **If I were to allow you to give me what I want—**. And this might lead very naturally to a stem such as **I learned to deny my wants when—**.

There is no set of rules to memorize for improvising stems. Listen as your partner completes the sentences, and help your partner to keep his or her process moving forward. This book is designed so that you will absorb the method—perhaps subconsciously more than consciously—by doing each exercise in sequence. New stems will come to you more and more easily with practice and experience.

Chapter 5

Understanding And Expressing Feelings—2

In the preceding chapter we focused on some negative feelings and emotions. Let us now begin a consideration of some positive ones. It is equally as important to understand joy as pain and to know how to communicate it appropriately.

❧ *Happiness* ❧

Sometimes I feel happy when

_____

_____

_____

_____

_____

_____

_____

_____

Sometimes when I'm happy, I

_____

_____

_____

_____

_____

_____

_____

_____

_____

One of the ways I sometimes hide my happiness is

_____

_____

_____

_____

_____

_____

_____

_____ 165

One of the ways my happiness comes out is

_____

_____

_____

_____

_____

_____

_____

_____

If I ever fully admitted when I feel happy

_____

_____

_____

_____

_____

_____

_____

_____

A better way to deal with my happiness might be

_____

_____

_____

_____

_____

_____

_____

_____

_____ 167

❧ *Reflections* ❧

You may be learning that we sometimes have difficulty in dealing with positive emotions, not just painful ones. Just as we do not always know how to handle fear or pain, so we do not always know how to handle joy. Take time to record your feelings, reactions, associations, and any tentative conclusions you have arrived at as of right now.

_____

_____

_____

_____

_____

_____

_____

_____

_____

_____

_____

❧ Reflections ❧

❧ Sexuality ❧

Sometimes I feel sexually excited when

_____

_____

_____

_____

_____

_____

_____

_____

_____

Sometimes when I'm sexually excited, I

_____

_____

_____

_____

_____

_____

_____

_____

_____

One of the ways I sometimes hide my sexual excitement is

_____

_____

_____

_____

_____

_____

_____

_____

_____

One of the ways my sexual excitement comes out is

_____

_____

_____

_____

_____

_____

_____

_____

_____

If I ever fully admitted when I feel sexually excited

_____

_____

_____

_____

_____

_____

_____

_____

_____

A better way to deal with my sexual excitement might be

_____

_____

_____

_____

_____

_____

_____

_____

_____

_____

❧ *Reflections* ❧

Pause. Review your endings. Remember, there is no assumption that everything you write is necessarily true. Some endings may be the implulse of the moment. Allow that. Try them on for size. When you read these endings again at a later date, some may feel more true than others, more enduring, more basic to who you really are

Take a pause here for any reflections you may have on your responses to the sentence stems on happiness and sex.

_____

_____

_____

_____

_____

_____

_____

_____

_____

_____

_____

❧ *Reflections* ❧

_____

_____

_____

_____

_____

_____

_____

_____

_____

_____

_____

_____

Now let us proceed to some new stems that should be done first here in the book by yourself and later, if possible, with a partner or a friend.

❧ *Allowing Others to See Who I Am* ❧

If I were willing to be vulnerable

_____

_____

_____

_____

_____

_____

_____

_____

_____

One of the things I wish people (you, my partner) knew about me is

_____

_____

_____

_____

_____

_____

_____

_____

If the child in me could speak, he/she might say

_____

_____

_____

_____

_____

_____

_____

_____

_____ 177

If I could be sure no one would hurt me

_____

_____

_____

_____

_____

_____

_____

_____

If I could be sure no one would laugh at me

_____

_____

_____

_____

_____

_____

_____

_____

_____

_____

_____

If I could admit how lonely I sometimes feel

_____

_____

_____

_____

_____

_____

_____

_____

_____

∼ *Reflections* ∼

Pause and rest. Review your endings. Breathe deeply and do your best to stay relaxed. Before proceeding to the final stems in this chapter, pause to record your reflections on this past set of sentence stems and your completions.

_____

_____

_____

_____

_____

_____

_____

_____

_____

_____

_____

_____

❧ Reflections ❧

❧ A Perspective on My Life ❧

All my life

_____

_____

_____

_____

_____

_____

_____

_____

_____

Ever since I was a child

_____

_____

_____

_____

_____

_____

_____

_____

_____

If I felt free to show my excitement

_____

_____

_____

_____

_____

_____

_____

_____

_____

If I allow myself to understand the things I've been saying here

_____

_____

_____

_____

_____

_____

_____

_____

_____

If any of what I am saying is true

_____

_____

_____

_____

_____

_____

_____

_____

_____

_____

_____

I'm beginning to suspect

_____

_____

_____

_____

_____

_____

_____

_____

_____

❧ *Reflections* ❧

What feelings are rising within you? What associations? What memories? What conclusions? What areas are you beginning to see you need to explore further?

_____

_____

_____

_____

_____

_____

_____

_____

_____

_____

_____

_____

❧ Reflections ❧

❧ Reflections ❧

_____

_____

_____

_____

_____

_____

_____

_____

_____

_____

_____

_____

_____

Chapter 6

Exploring Parental Influence On Relationships

Virtually from the beginning of life we receive messages from our parents concerning our bodies, our sexuality, and the nature of man/woman relationships. Sometimes these messages are explicit, more often they are implicit. Some of these messages we accepted as children, some we rejected.

We had already begun to explore the influence of parents on early development in Chapter Three. Here, we go deeper into that territory, focusing on parental influence as it specifically affects our intimate relationships today. The learnings and associations generated by the earlier work will be amplified here and will serve to stimulate the present exploration.

As always, the stems listed on the following pages are first to be done alone, then, if possible, with a partner or in a group.

❧ *Mother's Influence* ❧

Mother often gave me the feeling that I

_____

_____

_____

_____

_____

_____

_____

_____

One of Mother's ways of nurturing was to

_____

_____

_____

_____

_____

_____

_____

_____

_____

When Mother touched or held me, I felt

_____

_____

_____

_____

_____

_____

_____

_____

_____

Mother gave me the sense that my body was

_____

_____

_____

_____

_____

_____

_____

_____

_____

Mother gave me the sense that sex was

_____

_____

_____

_____

_____

_____

_____

_____

_____

_____

_____

Mother gave me a view of men as

_____

_____

_____

_____

_____

_____

_____

_____

_____

Mother gave me a view of women as

_____

_____

_____

_____

_____

_____

_____

_____

Mother gave me the sense that love was

_____

_____

_____

_____

_____

_____

_____

_____

_____

_____

_____

If Mother thought I was in a happy romantic relationship

_____

_____

_____

_____

_____

_____

_____

_____

One of the unspoken messages I got from Mother about love was

_____

_____

_____

_____

_____

_____

_____

_____

One of the unspoken messages I got from Mother about life was

_____

_____

_____

_____

_____

_____

_____

_____

_____

_____

_____

One of the unspoken messages I got from Mother about me was

_____

_____

_____

_____

_____

_____

_____

_____

_____

Mother gave me the sense that marriage was

_____

_____

_____

_____

_____

_____

_____

_____

One of the ways I'm like Mother is

(This stem is emphatically for men as much as for women.)

_____

_____

_____

_____

_____

_____

_____

_____

_____

_____

When I contemplate Mother's impact on my life and development

_____

_____

_____

_____

_____

_____

_____

_____

❧ *Reflections* ❧

Relax a moment. Meditate on what you have written. Allow whatever feelings that may arise in you simply to be there, without questioning, denial, or suppression. Take time for your reflections on Mother's influence, as disclosed in this section, before proceeding to the next set.

_____

_____

_____

_____

_____

_____

_____

_____

_____

_____

_____

_____

✣ Reflections ✣

❧ Father's Influence ❧

Father often gave me the feeling that I

_____

_____

_____

_____

_____

_____

_____

_____

One of Father's ways of nurturing was to

_____

_____

_____

_____

_____

_____

_____

_____

_____

When Father touched or held me, I felt

_____

_____

_____

_____

_____

_____

_____

_____

Father gave me the sense that my body was

_____

_____

_____

_____

_____

_____

_____

_____

_____

Father gave me the sense that sex was

_____

_____

_____

_____

_____

_____

_____

_____

_____

_____

_____

Father gave me a view of men as

_____

_____

_____

_____

_____

_____

_____

_____

_____

_____ 205

Father gave me a view of women as

_____

_____

_____

_____

_____

_____

_____

_____

Father gave me the sense that love was

_____

_____

_____

_____

_____

_____

_____

_____

_____

_____

If Father thought I was in a happy romantic relationship

_____

_____

_____

_____

_____

_____

_____

_____

_____

One of the unspoken messages I got from Father about love was

_____

_____

_____

_____

_____

_____

_____

_____

_____

One of the unspoken messages I got from Father about life was

_____

_____

_____

_____

_____

One of the unspoken messages I got from Father about me was

_____

_____

_____

_____

_____

_____

_____

Father gave me the sense that marriage was

_____

_____

_____

_____

_____

_____

_____

_____

One of the ways I'm like Father is

_____

_____

_____

_____

_____

_____

_____

_____

_____

_____

_____

When I contemplate Father's impact on my life and development

_____

_____

_____

_____

_____

_____

_____

_____

_____

◆❧ Reflections ❧◆

Pause here for reflections on what the preceding completions mean to you. Let your mind roam. Write down whatever comes to you.

_____

_____

_____

_____

_____

_____

_____

_____

_____

_____

_____

_____

Reflections

❧ Summing Up and Integrating ❧

I am beginning to feel

_____

_____

_____

_____

_____

_____

_____

_____

I am becoming aware

_____

_____

 _____

_____

_____

_____

_____

_____

I am beginning to suspect

_____

_____

_____

_____

_____

_____

_____

_____

_____ 215

✦ *Reflections* ✦

At this point, please read everything you have written from the beginning of the chapter. Remember that not all of it is necessarily true. If additional endings occur to you, write them in. Then pause to record your feelings and thoughts to this point in the space provided below.

_____

_____

_____

_____

_____

_____

_____

_____

_____

_____

_____

_____

_____

❧ Reflections ❧

❧ *Three Stems for People in Relationships* ❧

    If you are in a relationship at present, proceed to the next three sentence stems. If you're not in a relationship at present, use these stems to reflect on a past relationship.

Sometimes Mother speaks through my voice when I tell my partner

_____

_____

_____

_____

_____

_____

_____

_____

_____

_____

_____

Sometimes Father speaks through my voice when I tell my partner

_____

_____

_____

_____

_____

_____

_____

If I could separate my voice from my parents

_____

_____

_____

_____

_____

_____

_____

✑ Parents and Sex ✒

The next set of stems may strike you as strange or inapplicable. They may not seem to fit. Please open yourself to them, be willing to experiment. Don't back away from things you may not immediately understand or even think are true.

If it turns out I don't need my parents' permission to be a man/woman

_____

_____

_____

_____

_____

_____

_____

_____

_____

_____

_____

If it turns out I don't need my parents' permission to be a sexual being

_____

_____

_____

_____

_____

_____

_____

If I were fully willing to own and experience my sexuality

_____

_____

_____

_____

_____

_____

_____ 221

If I were fully accepting of my own body

_____

_____

_____

_____

_____

_____

_____

_____

If I were to admit how much I enjoy sex

_____

_____

_____

_____

_____

_____

_____

_____

_____

_____

If I didn't ever worry about my masculinity/femininity
   (I know you never worry, but do the endings anyway.)

_____

_____

_____

_____

_____

_____

_____

_____

Self-Acceptance

If I allowed myself just to enjoy who I am

_____

_____

_____

_____

_____

_____

_____

_____

_____

If I were willing to breathe deeply and feel my own power

_____

_____

_____

_____

If any of what I am saying is true

If I can accept whatever I have said without self-blame or self-criticism

_____

_____

_____

_____

_____

_____

_____

_____

As I grow more comfortable with accepting my own feelings

_____

_____

_____

_____

_____

_____

_____

_____

_____

_____

_____

As I grow more comfortable with expressing my inner thoughts

_____

_____

_____

_____

_____

_____

_____

_____

_____

⋙ Reflections ⋘

Pause and review your completions. You may have touched on material that can help you understand some of the transactions in your relationships. If you have a partner, you may want to stop here and do some of these sentence stems aloud in a two-person exercise. Don't feel that you have to say the same things you have written here. Allow new or additional material to emerge.

Please take time to record your reflections here before proceeding to the next set of stems.

_____

_____

_____

_____

_____

_____

_____

_____

_____

_____

❧ Reflections ❧

_____

_____

_____

_____

_____

_____

_____

_____

_____

_____

_____

_____

_____

_____

_____

❧ A Fresh Perspective on Parental Influences ❧

When I think of some of the ways Mother has influenced my attitudes toward men

_____

_____

_____

_____

_____

_____

_____

_____

When I think of some of the ways Mother has influenced my attitudes toward women

_____

_____

_____

_____

_____

_____

_____

_____

_____

_____

When I think of some of the ways Mother has influenced my attitudes toward my body

_____

_____

_____

_____

_____

_____

_____

_____

_____

When I think of some of the ways Mother has influenced my attitudes toward sex

_____

_____

_____

_____

_____

_____

_____

_____

When I think of some of the ways Mother has influenced my love life

_____

_____

_____

_____

_____

_____

_____

_____

_____

_____

If I allow myself to understand what I'm saying here

_____

_____

_____

_____

_____

_____

_____

_____

When I think of some of the ways Father has influenced my attitudes toward men

_____

_____

_____

_____

_____

_____

_____

When I think of some of the ways Father has influenced my attitudes toward women

_____

_____

_____

_____

_____

_____

_____

_____

_____

When I think of some of the ways Father has influenced my attitudes toward my body

_____

_____

_____

_____

_____

_____

_____

_____

When I think of some of the ways Father has influenced my attitudes toward sex

_____

_____

_____

_____

_____

_____

_____

_____

When I think of some of the ways Father has influenced my love life

_____

_____

_____

_____

_____

_____

_____

_____

_____

_____

If I allow myself to understand what I'm saying here

_____

_____

_____

_____

_____

_____

_____

_____

_____ 237

✃ *Reflections* ✃

Review your endings, and please record your reflections concerning Mother's and Father's influences. Remember, you may or may not have been aware of these influences in the past.

_____

_____

_____

_____

_____

_____

_____

_____

_____

_____

_____

_____

_____

Reflections

_____

_____

_____

_____

_____

_____

_____

_____

_____

_____

_____

_____

_____

_____

_____

❧ *Moving Toward Independence and Autonomy* ❧

If I choose to look at men with my own eyes

_____

_____

_____

_____

_____

_____

_____

_____

If I choose to look at women with my own eyes

_____

_____

_____

_____

_____

_____

_____

_____

If I choose to look at sex with my own eyes

_____

_____

_____

_____

_____

_____

_____

_____

_____

If I choose to look at myself with my own eyes

_____

_____

_____

_____

_____

_____

_____

_____

_____

As I become more comfortable with looking at things independently

_____

_____

_____

_____

_____

_____

_____

_____

_____

_____

_____

As I feel myself becoming free of negative influences from the past

_____

_____

_____

_____

_____

_____

_____

_____

_____

As I allow myself to experience all the positive feelings within me

_____

_____

_____

_____

_____

_____

_____

_____

One of the ways I might try to sabotage my positive feelings is

_____

_____

_____

_____

_____

_____

_____

_____

_____

_____

_____

One of the scary things about positive feelings is

_____

_____

_____

_____

_____

_____

_____

_____

As I become more and more comfortable with positive feelings

_____

_____

_____

_____

_____

_____

_____

_____

_____

As I become more and more comfortable with self-acceptance

_____

_____

_____

_____

_____

_____

_____

_____

_____

_____

_____

If I breathe deeply and allow myself to feel my own power

_____

_____

_____

_____

_____

_____

_____

_____

_____

Reflections

Reflections

A Cautionary Word

By now, if you have fully participated in the exercises in this book, the probability is very high that you have experienced a wide range of reactions: fear, anger, pain, grief, excitement, joy, shock, despair, euphoria, disorientation. To say it once more: all such reactions are entirely normal.

I would like to suggest, however, that you avoid taking any radical action on the basis of anything that may have developed for you so far in this book. For example, you may be feeling some anger over some of the sexual (or antisexual) messages you received from your parents, but it would not be a good idea to telephone your parents and start screaming at them about the harm they have done you. That is not what these exercises are about.

These exercises are to help you understand yourself and your partner better and to facilitate the process of communication between you. This may entail learning something about the roots of some of your present attitudes so that you can challenge and modify them if you do not like them. That is all.

These exercises are not a license to kill. Stated less theatrically, these exercises are not a license to indulge in an orgy of blaming. Blaming never facilitated anyone's growth. Blaming never nourished any love relationship. Blaming merely leaves the blamer feeling helpless, powerless, the victim of forces he or she can do nothing to alter. Blaming leaves the blamer in the role of a child. If you are able to participate in this book, you are no longer a child. Your life is in your own hands—if you choose to take responsibility. That is one of the main themes underlying this work.

Chapter 7

Learning To Express Appreciation And Love

It is clear that romantic love entails a desire to see and be seen, to appreciate and to be appreciated, to know and to be known, to explore and to be explored, to give visibility and to receive it. . . .

If we talk to people who have been happily in love for some time, we will often hear such statements as the following: 'He (she) makes me feel appreciated.' 'He (she) makes me feel better understood than I've ever felt in my life.' 'He makes me feel like a woman.' 'She makes me feel *seen*.'. . .

The ability to see and to communicate what one sees—that is, the ability to make the partner feel visible—is essential to the longevity of a romantic relationship.

The Psychology of Romantic Love

One of the characteristics of happy couples, or good friends, is that they know how to make each other feel visible, appreciated, loved. And yet, expressing love is often difficult for the same reason that seeking love is difficult. Fear. Fear of rejection. Fear of being abandoned. Fear of showing my feelings to anyone, even my lover. Fear of self-disclosure of any kind.

Such fears create a barrier that is seldom easy to overcome. Sentence completion can help.

❧ *Appreciation and Understanding* ❧

One of the things I would like to be valued and appreciated for is

_____

_____

_____

_____

_____

_____

_____

_____

One of the things I wish my partner (friend, family, colleagues) understood about me is

_____

_____

_____

_____

_____

_____

_____

_____

_____

    When doing a sentence, such as the above, aloud and face to face with a partner or friend, obviously the wording would be *One of the things I wish you understood about me is—*.

One of the things I appreciate about my partner (friend, family, colleagues) is

_____

_____

_____

_____

_____

_____

_____

_____

One of the qualities that first attracted me to my partner (friend, family, colleagues) was

_____

_____

_____

_____

_____

_____

_____

_____

_____

I feel loved and appreciated by my partner (friend, family, colleagues) when

_____

_____

_____

_____

_____

_____

_____

_____

_____

I feel sexually stimulated by my partner when he/she

_____

_____

_____

_____

_____

_____

_____

_____

_____

I feel especially happy with my partner (friend, family, colleagues) when

_____

_____

_____

_____

_____

_____

_____

_____

_____

If I were to communicate all of this to my partner (friend, family, colleagues)

_____

_____

_____

_____

 _____

_____

_____

_____

_____

_____

I am becoming aware

_____

_____

_____

_____

_____

_____

_____

_____

For Couples and Friends

The stems presented in this chapter lead implicitly to a two-person exercise. Until then, you have done only half the work and you have realized less than half the benefits. Try out the following stems, in the order given, when you are ready. "When you are ready" might mean later today or tomorrow; if you don't have any appointments in the next hour or so, it may as well be right now. (Keep in mind that any exercise in this book can produce fresh results when gone through again at a later time and in different circumstances.) As before, each person takes a turn giving the stem aloud and listening attentively to the other's completions.

One of the things I appreciate about you is—
One of the qualities that first attracted me to you was—
I feel loved and appreciated by you when you—
I feel sexually stimulated by you when you—

It is important to notice what we feel when we are expressing our completions, and also when our partner or friend is expressing completions to us. Can we express love with comfort and grace? Can we accept love with comfort and grace?

Or do we feel uneasy, anxious, undeserving? These are feelings to be shared: confiding them, trusting someone to help you with them always deepens intimacy. Sentence completion can further enrich the discussion:

As I express these thoughts and feelings to you—
As I sit here listening to you—

Two people who want to deal with a sense of psychological invisibility may find these stems useful:

I feel invisible when you—
I might feel more visible if you would—
One of the things I would like you to value and appreciate about me is—
One of the things I wish you better understood about me is—

Sometimes we withhold appreciation and love because of unexpressed hurt or anger. It may be fruitful to experiment with:

Sometimes I withhold expressions of appreciation when—
The good thing about allowing you to feel invisible and unappreciated is—
If I were to make you feel more visible and appreciated—
By keeping you uncertain as to my feelings about you, I—
By causing you to wonder if I really love you, I—
If I were more willing to let you see how much you matter to me—
If I were more willing to allow you to know what I love about you—

This kind of sequence should conclude with stems such as:

I am becoming aware—
I am beginning to suspect—
If I allow myself to understand what I am saying—
When I am ready to understand fully what I have been saying—
Right now it seems obvious—

It isn't necessary to use all of these stems, but a minimum of two will almost certainly be productive and illuminating.

Couples and friends who are willing to come this far *are communicating*.

To quote once more from *The Psychology of Romantic Love*:

For men and women who are not afraid to love, who are not obsessed with fear of rejection, one of the great pleasures of being in love is the pleasure of making the partner feel more visible to him or herself, more self-aware and more self-appreciative. One of the great pleasures is to lead the partner to deeper and deeper levels of self-discovery.

Such an attitude originates in the fact of being truly *fascinated* with the partner, of *wanting* to see and understand this other human being, and of realizing that this is a process without end. Contrary to the cliche that 'love is blind,' love has the power of seeing with the greatest clarity and to the greatest depth, because the motivation is there, the inspiration is there. Those whom we do not love we do not ordinarily look at closely or for such long periods of time.

Sometimes I will hear a person say, 'But I understand my partner totally. There is nothing new to see or discover. How could there be? We have been together for ten years!' A person who speaks in this manner is revealing something else entirely, not about the partner but about the self: an attitude of mental passivity that commonly is manifest in other areas of life as well. It is never true that there is 'nothing more to understand.' There is always more, if only because a person is engaged in a constant process of unfolding. And further, our active desire to *see* our partner and our ability to do so with fresh eyes *encourages* the process of growth and unfolding within him or her.

◆ *Reflections* ◆

Take time to record your thoughts and feelings as of this point. What conclusions are you coming to? What are you learning? What area or aspect of communication do you feel you need to think about further? What would you like to change about the way you and your partner communicate at present?

_____

_____

_____

_____

_____

_____

_____

Reflections

❧ Reflections ❧

Chapter 8

Understanding Self-Acceptance

It is natural that different readers will respond differently to the exercises in this book. Some may respond eagerly; some may respond skeptically. Some may commit themselves to full participation; some may withdraw and stop after a few half-hearted efforts. Some may allow their sentence completions to lead them into deeper and deeper levels of awareness; some may fight the process and remain closer to the surface with the known, the familiar, the safe.

Some may allow themselves to say whatever comes to mind; some may feel the need to impose censorship. Some may persevere, even when sentence completions arise that are dismaying, confusing, disorienting; others may panic and stop at the first sentence completion that seems dangerous or threatening. All of these responses are understandably human.

I wish there were some way for me to be present while each of you worked with these sentence stems, so I could guide you through difficult moments, encourage a spirit of openness and self-acceptance, encourage an attitude of self-compassion, and improvise new stems that might help you out of what might momentarily feel like catastrophic realizations. But since I cannot literally be with you, I want to at least leave you with a few final observations and suggestions.

Perhaps the single most important concept in doing sentence-completion work—or, for that matter, in living your life—is that of *self-acceptance*. What does self-acceptance mean? To accept yourself, to accept what you are, is to refuse to disown or deny or repress any part of your experience—your thoughts, feelings, emotions, desires, aversions, actions. The simplest form of disowning is to make yourself unaware of unwanted elements of your experience, to refuse to perceive them. But there are other forms of disowning, less readily recognized.

You may note one of your feelings and reactions and then tell yourself, "That's wrong! That can't possibly be my attitude!" You may begin to be aware, then abort the process by convincing yourself you are mistaken; and the awareness surrenders and vanishes.

Or you may become aware of some emotion to which you react with shame or embarrassment, and you apologize to yourself or others, saying, in effect, "I know this is silly" or "I know this is awful." You may be eager to put as much psychological distance as possible between you and your feeling, aggressively forbidding integration of the fact that at a given point in time, this particular feeling or emotion was your way of experiencing some aspect of your existence.

Or you may become aware of an emotion that is painful or threatening and proceed to intellectualize, saying, "Now this is an interesting phenomenon! I wonder what causes a person to have such an experience? It really makes one feel dreadful." By a flight into impersonality, by inducing a state of dissociation in yourself, you escape from the awareness that the emotion you are experiencing *is your own* and it says something about you and your condition.

To accept yourself is to accept what you are without censorship, to let yourself be fully aware of your thoughts, feelings, emotions, desires, aversions, actions—to let them be fully real, to accept responsibility for them, to acknowledge them as your own, to accept the fact that they are all expressions of your self *at the time they occur.*

"Accepting what one is" requires that you approach the contemplation of your experience with neither approval nor disapproval but rather with an attitude that makes such concepts irrelevant: the desire to be aware.

You are not obligated to like or to want to retain every feeling, emotion, experience you take note of. Self-acceptance is not the equivalent of "desiring to remain unchanged."

And neither is self-acceptance tantamount to acting out every feeling or impulse you experience. Action requires judgment and discrimination. Self-acceptance pertains to an attitude of openness toward your own experience, an allowing of your feelings and emotions, an attitude of respect toward the self.

Self-acceptance entails not fighting the moment, not fighting your immediate awareness, not fighting your feelings, emotions, or other responses. Self-acceptance means being willing to let emotions in, relaxing into whatever is the reality of the moment, and being a witness to it.

When I endeavor to communicate the concept of self-acceptance to clients or to students at my Intensive Workshops, I am sometimes met with the protest, "But I don't like the way I am. I want to be different."

The person will say, for example, "I don't like to be afraid of what people think of me. I hate that part of myself. I wish I could get rid of it." Or, "I'm ashamed of the fact that I can't say 'no' to anyone who wants to sleep with me. I loathe myself for being that way. Am I supposed to approve of it?" Or, "I see people I admire, people who are strong, self-confident, self-assertive. That's the way I want to be. Why should I accept being a nonentity?"

I have already noted one of the fallacious assumptions implicit in these statements: to accept that I am what I am is not to approve of every aspect of my personality. Further, to accept myself is not to forbid the possibility of change. On the contrary, *self-acceptance is the precondition of change.*

If I deny my feelings, if I block my inner experiences, I keep myself in a perpetual state of conflict and tension. I generate that condition known as self-alienation. If, instead, I permit myself to experience and acknowledge my denied feelings, I reeastablish contact with myself, I make it possible for my unwanted feelings to be discharged, and I unblock the integrative process by means of which my internal well-being is preserved. I discuss this process in some detail in *The Disowned Self.*

To quote from that book:

A man complained that he had lost all sexual desire for his wife, while at the same time insisting that he loved her deeply; he professed to be utterly bewildered by his sexual indifference. I was inclined to believe him. Knowing that a damming up of sexual feeling is often a consequence of the repression of anger and hurt, I suggested that—without attacking or denouncing *her,* but speaking only of his own feelings and reactions—he face her, (she was present at the interview), and utter some sentences beginning with the words "I get angry when . . ." He did so, and very shortly an unexpected (to him) torrent of outraged feelings began to pour forth. It soon became evident that the anger was covering a good deal of unacknowledged pain. I suggested that he utter some sentences beginning with the words "I am hurt that . . ." He did so, and waves of previously unacknowledged pain began flowing into his awareness.

Whenever he attempted to shift from describing his own feelings to making statements about his wife's imagined motives, psychology and so forth, he was asked to abstain from doing so and to confine his statements to descriptions of his own feelings, and to descriptions of the grossly observable *facts* to which his feelings were experienced as a response (facts available to his sight and hearing, rather than "facts" he imagined to be taking place inside her consciousness). One of the most prevalent forms of seeking to escape from one's inner experience is to switch one's focus to another person, and proceed to make statements about that person's presumed intentions, feelings, moral worth, or whatever. If, for instance, a person does not wish to face his own hurt—perhaps because he experiences it as humiliating or an indication of weakness—he may seek to escape from it by attacking the character of the person he regards as responsible and dealing with that person's *imagined* psychology rather than his own *actual* psychology.

Within a few hours after the couple left my office, my client's sexual feeling for his wife returned in full intensity—as he reported at our next session.

In forbidding himself to experience and confront his anger and hurt, he had effectively cut off *all* his feelings toward her— he had anesthetized himself emotionally—which is, unfortunately, an extremely common pattern between partners in a marital relationship. Further, on the subconscious level, his wife had become too associated with pain and resentment; as a consequence, his sexual capacity "went on strike." Whenever a person complains of lack of sexual feeling for his partner, a valuable line of inquiry is to look for unexpressed anger, resentment and hurt. Contrary to the "don't-rock-the-boat" theory of marriage, the communication of angry or hurt feelings—when *not* accompanied by an attack on the worth of the other party—is one of the most effective means of reestablishing intimacy as well as of releasing and strengthening sexual passion.

By allowing yourself to say whatever comes to mind in doing sentence-completion work, and by allowing yourself full access to your own feelings and emotions, you facilitate the possibility of new learnings, of transcending outworn attitudes, of growing to new levels of self-awareness while at the same time deepening the intimacy of your contact with your partner.

It is inevitable that at one point or another frightening or dismaying thoughts will come to you. Let them come. If they are true and enduring, you need to know them. If they are distortions of your real attitudes, experiencing them fully will allow you to gain a new per-

UNDERSTANDING
SELF-ACCEPTANCE

spective on them and reach a clearer understanding of what you actually think and feel.

Whether sentence-completion work brings us closer to our partner or brings us to the realization that our relationship no longer serves us, we are better served by knowing the truth rather than remaining in darkness.

In my own experience, sentence completion has led far more often to the revitalizing of relationships than to their end.

Any experiment with honesty and intimacy entails risk. That is in the nature of life. But what is love, what is a relationship, what is marriage, without honesty and intimacy?

Sometimes it is difficult for us to understand that on our way to truth we need the freedom to exaggerate our feelings, to overstate negative reactions. This is a freedom we should give ourselves and our partner in the process of sentence completion. Never assume that because some sentence completions sound ominous, they are the final word on the subject. They may be only way stations on the road to a deeper truth that may not disclose itself until later. For example, you may feel the need to express some fairly harsh resentments against your partner before you can once again open the door to your feelings of love, for reasons already explained in the preceding pages. You and your partner need the courage to accept such a possibility and to respect the steps of the process by which estrangement can be replaced by a new and more meaningful intimacy. In work of this kind, the biggest enemy is a fear that stops the process before it is completed.

I would not feel confident in offering this technique to the general public had I not already received so much feedback from clients and students who, for some years now, have been experimenting with the technique on their own at home and, as I said in the opening of this book, have been reporting some marvelously successful results. Their experience has given me the confidence that persons can derive value from this technique without the assistance of a teacher, guide, or therapist. I would be very pleased and grateful if you would care to write me of your own experience with sentence-completion work. I would especially be interested in any difficulties or problems that arise so that I may address myself to them in future writing. (Please address your communications to P.O. Box 4009, Beverly Hills, CA 90213.)

I conduct two-and-a-half day seminars, called Intensive Work-shops, in the areas of self-esteem enhancement, personal transformation, and man/woman relationships. Although I use many other processes in these Intensives besides sentence completion, there is a very real sense in which coming to the end of this book is like coming to the end of an Intensive Workshop. You have almost certainly been bombarded by more stimuli, originating chiefly in your own responses, than you can possibly assimilate or deal with on a purely conscious level. A large part of the job of assimilation and integration is handled, as I have already indicated, at the subconscious level of mind. But the process is far from completed at this point. Just as the effects of an Intensive go on reverberating for many weeks and months after the weekend experience itself, just as the seeds planted in that setting often sprout a long time after the event, so do this book and your many responses constitute a similar kind of seeding—of you and by you. The effects of your work here extend into the indefinite future. There is simply no way to see the end of the road at this point—and no need to.

More than one student of an Intensive has contacted me many months after the event and said, in effect, "I thought you were exaggerating when you spoke of planting time-delay capsules that would keep popping open in the mind at later dates. But that's precisely what my experience has been. New revelations, new insights keep popping up. I notice positive changes in my behavior after the fact; by the time I notice, the change has already begun."

I will presume to make the same prediction here: long after you have set this book aside, the seeds you have planted in your own mind will continue to grow, enriching your self-understanding and enriching your relationships. You can contribute to this development by redoing the exercises in a separate notebook at a later date. If you do that, without rereading what you have written here, I venture to say you will find yourself coming up in many cases with interestingly different completions. And those very differences can help you become aware of your growth since finishing this book.

And if, along the way, you become agitated by something you are saying or feeling, allow me to say to you here precisely what I would say if you were at one of my Intensives: "Breathe. Don't fight the feeling, relax into it. Allow it in. Allow it to flow through you. Be a witness to your own experience. Don't demand that it be different than it is. Don't fight the moment. Don't fight what your organism needs to feel right now. Breathe. Allow. Observe. Allow the experience to happen. Let yourself be. It's not disaster waiting for you at the end of the road, but joy—and the realization of how much you have never had to fear."

Chapter 9

Breaking Barriers

To the extent that it is possible for you, I would like you to temporarily "let go" of everything you have written in this book. At some subconscious level of mind, you will doubtless continue to be occupied with what you have written, but at least on a conscious level, I invite you to relax for a while, to rest, and to meditate on the simple examples I offer on the following pages. They dramatize some of the key issues of this book.

It's likely that somewhere in these pages you will encounter issues and situations to which you can relate personally. And even if you don't match the particulars, the methods involved in these stories are usable by everyone.

Carla asked Max if there was anything she could do that would help him to be more open in expressing his feelings.

"It's my problem," Max muttered. "I'll just have to figure out a way to solve it."

"Honey, can you tell me anything about how I can help?"

Max looked at her, muste and helpless.

Having participated in a number of my Intensive Workshops, they were familiar with sentence completion. Carla had an inspiration. **"One of the ways you could help me talk about my feelings is—."**

"I really feel blank," Max answered.

"Please try." Carla paused, repeated the stem again, and this time Max answered.

One of the ways you could help me talk about my feelings is—

by sitting still when I'm trying to tell you something.

by understanding that sometimes I'm very scared.

by not overwhelming me with your words.

by not always giving me lectures.

by not always telling me, "I told you so."

by letting me ramble.

by not acting like my mother.

by not going off on your own feelings when I'm trying to talk about mine.

by not telling me I shouldn't be feeling what I'm feeling.

by not interrupting as soon as I begin to show anger.

by not always correcting me.

by listening.

Carla was stunned. Max felt pleased with himself. "How about you trying one?" he suggested. **"The good thing about making it hard for you to express your feelings is—."**
Carla looked at him, gulped, and began.
The good thing about making it hard for you to express your feelings is—

I stay in control.

I don't have to hear anything upsetting.

I have something to complain about.

I get to feel neglected.

I keep you off balance.

I am the expert on feelings and emotions.

"Okay," said Max. "Now I guess we can talk."
Not an end. A beginning.

Brad complained that Geraldine seemed uninterested in his sexual wants during their lovemaking. Geraldine said she was very interested but had trouble deciphering his signals. When Geraldine asked Brad to talk about his sexual wants, he became blocked.
"Maybe I don't take enough responsibility," Brad thought aloud. "Is it possible I'm laying this whole trip on you unfairly?" Facing Geraldine, he improvised a stem for himself to complete.

One of the ways I make it difficult for you to give me what I want is—

I don't tell you what I want.

often I don't let myself know what I want.

I act as if I don't want anything.

I'm so busy moving around, I don't give you a chance to catch up with me.

I communicate discomfort when you give it to me.

I expect you to know without my telling you.

I keep you at a distance by always being the one who gives to you sexually.

Paying close attention, Geraldine suggested a new stem, and Brad completed it.

The scary thing about expressing what I want is—

you may not care.

you may not respond.

I'll have to admit I have wants.

I'll be too vulnerable.

I'll feel too exposed.

not getting what I want would hurt too much.

I feel defenseless.

I feel vulnerable.

I'll be out of control.

I'll have to let it in that you love me.

it's too intimate

Here Brad stopped. "Wait a minute. I want to go deeper into that."

If I were to tell you how scared I am of intimacy—

I wouldn't be so scared anymore.

what a relief!

I'd have to tell you how alone I felt growing up.

I'd have to tell you how much I need you.

all the walls would crumble.

I'd feel like a raw nerve.

I'd feel free.

we'd have a better marriage.

I'd know that intimacy is what I've always wanted.

you'd understand me better.

I'd understand myself better.

I wouldn't feel resentful over your not being a mind reader.

we'd laugh.

I could always feel like I'm feeling right now!

No miracle has been accomplished. But a wall has been breached.

Charles and Marie had been experimenting for over a year with sentence completion. It had become something of a family institution. Sometimes they used the process playfully, as in **One of the things I wouldn't mind having for dinner is—**.

One day they decided to look into why Charles kept putting off agreed-on household chores. Charles began with **The bad thing about doing household chores is—**

I don't feel like it.

Mother did all that when I was growing up.

(Laughing) I gave at the office.

doing it makes me feel mad.

I feel like I'm giving in to you.

As is often the case with people who are experienced in sentence completion, the work went fast. Charles shifted to integrating stems. **I'm beginning to suspect—**

I resent doing household work.

I never thought it was a man's job.

sometimes I feel persecuted.

sometimes I resent you

I'm a little childish about all of this.

if I'm bothered about something, I should tell you in plain English.

if I make an agreement that seems fair, I'd better stick to it.

what do I think I am, a Princess?

Right now it seems obvious—

I really do hate household work.

I've got a lot of anger over this subject.

I wonder if I was right to agree in the first place.

boy, am I ambivalent!

this is where a grown man stops fooling around and just does it!

I would feel better if I did it.

talking this way is relaxing.

this isn't funny anymore.

I'm really feeling a little ashamed of myself.

it's time to stop procrastinating and get my act together.

I really am sorry.

An uphill climb still lay ahead. Old habits die hard. But sentence completion had brought into focus what had not been in focus before.

Sometimes Marilyn was passionate sexually, sometimes she was strained and inhibited. She and her husband Gary attempted to understand why, but their conversations led nowhere.

"I know you enjoy sex," said Gary, "only sometimes you won't let yourself."

They began working with sentence completion. Marilyn supplied endings for the stem **If I were to admit how much I really enjoy sex—**

I'd be happier.

I'd wonder what Mother would think.

I'd belong to myself.

I wouldn't be my parents' good little girl anymore.

I'd make you happier.

I'd feel freer.

I'd have to admit I'm not a child anymore.

I'd stop hurting both of us.

If it's true that I enjoy sex whether I admit it or not—

then who am I kidding?

then I might as well let us be happy.

then I'm foolish.

then my own judgment has got to start counting for more.

then what's the big deal?

then it's time to stop pretending.

then what have I been doing to both of us?

this is going to take getting used to!

Gary suggested a follow-up stem for her to experiment with. **If I were willing to admit I take pleasure in my body—**

I could tell you how much I love making love with you.

maybe I'd feel guilty.

I'd have to realize I'm a woman.

I might be condemned.

I might feel free.

I might realize I've been a fool.

I might be accused of flaunting myself sexually.

I might realize only you and I matter.

I would be telling the truth.

I would be setting us free.

The next week in their group therapy session, Marilyn declared, "I've got progress to report and problems to work on. I think I'm almost there—and I need a push to get me through." (Which of course evoked from her therapist the sentence stem **If it turns out I don't need you to teach me what I already know—**.

Pauline and Jeff had had many fights about money. He felt she was extravagant. She felt he was overcontrolling money that belonged to them both. Each of them conceded that the other might be right, but neither could truly understand the other's motives or even discuss the problem intelligently.

When they were introduced to sentence completion, Pauline worked with the stem **The good thing about spending money extravagantly is—**

it makes me feel loved.

it's a source of pleasure.

it gets me out of the house.

it makes me feel we're better off than we are.

it makes me feel important.

it relieves the strain of not having anything to do with my time.

it upsets you and gets you talking to me.

Then Jeff took a turn. **The good thing about overcontrolling how much money you can spend is—**

it keeps you dependent on me.

it's a release from my anger over your not having a job.

I feel in control.

I'm the boss.

maybe it'll force you to think about doing something with your time.

Here are some additional stems for couples who want to explore any difficulties they have concerning money:

Money, to me, means—

When I complain about your attitude toward money, what I am really trying to say is—

It might be easier for us to agree about money if only you would—

If I were to respect your preferences about spending as much as I respect my own—

Maybe I would feel differently about money if only—

Sometimes when we fight about money, what I think we are really trying to tell each other is—

Janet and Peter had lived together for two years and were trying to decide whether or not they should marry. They had difficulty articulating their reasons. They knew their feelings were ambivalent. Janet began using sentence stems that approached the problem from the opposite direction.

The scary thing about marriage is—

I may not belong to myself anymore.

I may lose my independence.

almost all the married couples I've seen are miserable.

how can I be sure Peter will be faithful?

it hurts too much if it breaks up.

I don't want the kind of life Mother had.

marriage means admitting how much I really care.

The good thing about getting married is—

I really love you.

I want us to be fully committed to each other.

I want to spend my life with you.

I can't see myself with anyone else.

I love being with you.

I'm happier with you than with anyone I've ever known.

Then Peter responded to the same stems.

The bad thing about getting married is—

what if we don't make it?

I don't want to fail.

I'm not sure it'll be forever.

marriage is so conventional.

everybody gets married.

I don't want to lose the romance between us.

I would feel so rotten if anything were to go wrong.

The good thing about getting married is—

I love you.

I know you're the woman for me.

when I picture us married, I feel I'm where I belong.

I feel fulfilled with you.

Janet's endings were very much like Peter's when they decided to work with **Marriage to me means—**. Her first responses were:

a final choice.

a commitment.

what I've longed for all my life.

sharing my life with another person.

happiness . . . and fear.

something solemn.

something I really want with you, if I have the courage to admit it.

Peter was feeling euphoric until he heard Janet's next ending:

"Marriage to me means having children"

When Janet saw the expression on his face, she deliberately chose to repeat herself. "Marriage to me means having children."
Peter's face fell. His euphoria was replaced by despair. When he

gave Janet the stem **If Peter refuses to have children—,** her endings were what he had dreaded:

I'd always resent him.

I'd have to face the fact that some of our values are different.

I couldn't see myself married to him.

I'd feel crushed.

They had learned sentence completion at an Intensive Workshop. At this moment sentence completion led them to the decision to seek counseling.

Larry recognized he had a habit of doing things that would make Monica angry, small acts of thoughtlessness or inconsideration that they had discussed many times, such as borrowing her car without asking or bringing home surprise guests for dinner. "I feel," Monica said to him one day, "that you get some satisfaction out of keeping me off-balance and angry so much of the time." "Why would I do that?" Larry asked. "Does it feel like it could be true?" To find out, Larry gave endings for this stem. **The good thing about making you angry is—**

it makes me feel persecuted.

I feel like a bad boy.

I feel hurt.

I feel punished.

it keeps us from being happy.

Monica introduced another stem for him suggested by these completions. **The good thing about keeping us unhappy is—**

I don't deserve to be happy.

Mother and Father weren't happy.

if I were to be happier than Father, he would feel betrayed, abandoned, hurt, humiliated.

I would be bad.

Then Larry remembered something he had learned at an Intensive about people who spend their whole lives trying to prove they are good boys or good girls—at the expense of their happiness as adults. He switched to this stem. **One of the ways I keep myself a good boy is—**

by being bad.

by being a bad boy.

by doing things to anger you.

by showing Father, "See, I haven't abandoned you."

by punishing myself.

by getting you to punish me.

"So the only way you can be a good boy is by being a bad boy," said Monica.

"I wonder how to—" Larry began, then he switched to a stem. **If I—were to allow myself to be happy—**

I'd treat you better.

I'd have to grow up.

I'd be responsible for my own life.

there would have to be distance between me and my parents.

it would be a new beginning.

I could try it and see if I liked it.

I'd be more considerate of you.

I'd let my love for you show itself more.

I wouldn't keep sabotaging us.

I wouldn't keep hurting you.

you'd see what I really feel for you.

I wouldn't keep you so confused.

I'd give you a sane reality.

I'd know that I don't have to be like my father.

I'd know that his life doesn't have to be mine.

I'd have more self-respect.

Having attended one of my Intensive Workshops on self-esteem, Jerry, age eighteen, and Linda, his mother of forty-one, were trying a few weeks later to explore further some of the difficulties in their relationship. Linda had learned a good deal about parenting at the Intensive, but Jerry remained adamantly unresponsive when she made an effort to reach out to him. He did agree to participate in sentence completion if Linda gave her endings first.

One of the things I'd like you to know about me is—

sometimes being a parent scares me.

I don't always know what to do.

I love you very much.

I get very angry at you sometimes.

I'm not even sure I like you sometimes.

when we're talking and not getting anywhere, I feel inadequate.

I wonder what I can do to make you see how much I care.

I wonder if it's too late.

I resent your resentment of me.

I'm tired of feeling guilty toward you.

I wonder what you get out of being so cold.

I want so much to close the gap between us.

After several minutes of floundering for a stem that Jerry might use, she was surprised to hear her son suggest one and then rapidly complete it. **One of the ways I'm getting back at you is—**

by pretending not to see when you reach out.

by remaining aloof.

by acting indifferent.

by showing you I had a good time with Dad.

by laughing at lot with Dad and always being very serious with you.

by pushing you away.

by making sarcastic remarks.

by looking at you as if to tell you I don't believe anything you're saying.

Linda offered a follow-up stem for him to answer.
The good thing about keeping you at a distance is—

you'll know how much you hurt me.

I won't have to feel my own pain.

I won't have to trust you.

I won't have to take any more chances with you.

I can make you suffer.

I can make you jealous of Dad.

I can make you fight with Dad for my affection.

I can let you know I'll never forgive you for all the times you were too busy for me when I was little.

I can make you feel you're never going to be off the hook.

I can have revenge.

"You look like you want to cry," said Linda. Jerry looked steadily at the floor, as if to say there would be nothing more from him. His mother lifted his chin so that once again his eyes were seeing hers. **"If my unshed tears could speak—"** she began.
He responded. **If my unshed tears could speak—**

I'd tell you how hurt I was.

I'd tell you how lonely I was.

I'd tell you how much I wanted a mother.

I'd yell and scream.

I'd say cruel things to you.

I'd hug you.

I'd let go of this anger.

I'd breathe more easily.

I'd smile at you sometimes.

I'd admit I know that holding down a job and looking after the family was hard for you, too.

I'd let you see how much I need you.

I'd be taking a chance.

I'd be scared.

I'd hope you wouldn't be frightened and run away.

I'd want you to be there.

I'd want you to know.

I'd need for you to understand.

we could be friends.

I wouldn't be cruel.

Some of the most inspiring stories that have come back to me from clients and students have been of this kind—not between lovers but between parents and children. The possibilities are endless.

Nathaniel and his wife Devers had finished writing *The Romantic Love Question & Answer Book,* and the subject turned to vacations.

"It's odd," said Devers. "When we're away on vacation, you're almost always happy and enjoy yourself. And yet you almost always resist going away. I wonder why."

"It's been that way as long as I can remember," said Nathaniel. "I think I'm overimbued with the idea that work is life. That's one explanation. Another is that I'm basically lazy and know that I don't dare stop working because of how hard it will be to get started again. Maybe both explanations are true."

Devers said, **"The bad thing about going on vacation is—"** "Okay," said Nathaniel. **The bad thing about going on vacation is—**

I'll feel like I'm loafing.

I'll wonder if I'll have time to write all the books I want to write.

I won't feel as much in control as I feel at my desk.

I'll be so happy I'll explode.

I'll be enjoying the present so much I won't ever want to go back to work.

I'll be enjoying you so much I won't have patience for anything or anyone else.

Devers, who knows when not to let up, said **"When I allow myself to surrender to happiness—"**
Nathaniel responded:

I feel proud of myself.

I know that this is what life is really all about.

I wonder why it's taken me so long to get here.

I feel serene.

I feel at peace.

I realize I've outgrown the teenager who used to think that nothing is as romantic as struggle.

I realize that there is nothing higher than this moment, right now, right here.

Devers and Nathaniel went away for a marvelous vacation, and Nathaniel spent scarcely any time at all thinking about the book he would write next. It was to be a book about communication and sentence completion.

The right sequence of sentence stems can lead us to the full resolution of a problem, but this is not always the case. More often than not, sentence completion is not an ending but a beginning. A sublime beginning.

Sentence completion can give voice to unshed tears, to disowned hurt, to suppressed rage. It can give voice to tenderness, passion, and love. It can be an awakening to ourselves and to those we love.

But it is not magic. It does not operate successfully without good will and a genuine desire to grow, to learn, and to expand awareness, contact, intimacy.

It is not a substitute for courage and honesty. Nothing is.

If it is a doorway into the self, so it is a doorway to union with another human being.

Open the door and walk through.

In conclusion, I offer a final sentence stem and some endings that may speak to you and for you.

If you could hear what I cannot say—

you would know that it's not indifference but hurt and anger that sometimes make me silent.

you might be frightened by the violence that would come out of me.

you would know the love inside of me struggling to find a voice.

you would know I sometimes feel like a child.

you would see the teenager in me.

you would understand the tension in my mouth and chest.

we would wonder at the time we wasted.

we could begin to talk.

you would see the excitement I'm so often afraid to show.

you would hear my laughter.

you would know that when I'm cruel, it's because I'm afraid of losing you.

you would know that when I'm remote, it's because I love you so much I don't know what to say or do.

you would know how terrified I am when you cut off from me.

you'd see that I'm shy.

I'd have to admit my needs and wants.

we would let go of the past and open to the present.

you would know me.

I would know myself.

you would hear good-bye.

you would hear hello.

maybe we would be ready to be in love.

Appendix:

❧ ——————— ❧

The Most Widely Useful Sentence-Completions Presented In This Book

It might be easier for us to agree about money if only you
would   *276*
If I were to respect your preferences about spending as much as I
respect my own   *276*
Maybe I would feel differently about money if only   *276*
Sometimes when we fight about money, what I think we are really
trying to tell each other is   *276*

ADDITIONAL STEMS FOR COUPLES

One of the ways I sometimes hurt you is   *162*
One of the ways I sometimes make you angry is   *162*
One of the ways I sometimes frustrate you is   *162*
One of the ways I sometimes make it difficult for you to love me
is   *162*
One of the ways I sometimes make it difficult for you to give me
what I want is   *162*

ABOUT THE AUTHOR

Also author of *The Psychology of Self-esteem, Breaking Free, The Disowned Self, The Psychology of Romantic Love,* and *The Romantic Love Question & Answer Book,* Nathaniel Branden is a pioneer in his studies of self-esteem, personal transformation, and man/woman relationships. Dr. Branden is in private practice in Los Angeles and lives in Lake Arrowhead, California.

As director of the Biocentric Institute in Los Angeles, he offers Intensive Workshops throughout the United States in self-esteem and man/woman relationships. He also conducts professional training workshops for mental health professionals in his approach to personal growth and development.

Communications to Dr. Branden or requests for information about his various lectures, seminars, and Intensive Workshops should be addressed to The Biocentric Institute, P.O. Box 4009, Beverly Hills, CA 90213.